TESTIMONIALS

Meeting Steve (and attending his training) was a life-changing event for me. When we met in 2003, I had five years of sales experience and, while I had been successful, I needed someone to help guide me – and I'm so very lucky that person was Steve! I had so much more to learn! Steve's programs helped me to find ways to say what I was feeling – he really pushed me to step outside of my comfort zone. The way I ask questions, the way I interact with people, this was influenced by him. Steve also helped me to be more present when interacting with my customers. I find that when I have a lot going on, a lot of distractions, I will find myself reminding myself of his words. Before every meeting, I will take time to think about what I want to accomplish, and envision the outcome.

Susan Diorio, Territory Account Manager

I've had great success with Steve. Each coaching session recharges the enthusiasm batteries. In the past one and a half years, Steve's coaching has accelerated my goals by three years. In case you're a "fact finder," my annual sales have increased by 154% over the past 12 months even in a "down economy." I would strongly recommend Steve Lentini as a coach for anyone who wants to be enthusiastic about his or her future.

Jeff Ferreira, President, Noonan Painting

Steve Lentini was an excellent speaker at our National Sales Meeting. Steve did some real homework talking to different reps and managers before the meeting that allowed him to make a connection with our team. Steve hit on and reinforced the topics that were important to me while bringing in his own perspective and experience. I give Steve a solid thumbs up and positive recommendation for any sales leader considering him for a speaking engagement.

With regard,

Eric Steen, Chief Executive Officer.

I had high expectations for Steve at our National Sales Meeting and he delivered! He was extremely well prepared and was able to put together a speech that hit on all the points we were looking to cover. We wanted a presentation that would not just make our team better at selling, but more importantly, make them better people. The feedback from the team was 100% positive and I look forward to having Steve be part of our sales training program in the future.

Richard Diorio, CEO, Infusystem.

Table of Contents

Testimonials
Foreword 1 A few thoughts to prepare the ground 4
Foreword 2 Get ready to change 4
Section 1 4
Seeds of the Sale 4
Preface 4
Chapter 1: Stay Certain of Success 4
Chapter 2: Ask them what their needs are and make a purchase happen 4
Chapter 3: Be Upfront and Go for No 4
Chapter 4: Give more but don't over promise 4
Chapter 5: Make relationship, stand in their shoes and get to know them better 4
Chapter 6: Detach from outcomes 4
Chapter 7: Don't Settle for Less 4
Chapter 8: Develop a System to follow 4
Chapter 9: Social Media – Get it Right. 4
Chapter 10: Multi-Level Marketing Sales 4
Section 2 4
Seeds of Success 4
Chapter 11: Use and understand the 4
Chapter 12: Set Time and boundaries and sell only the best of the best. 4
Chapter 13: Deal cheerfully with objections and complaints. 4
Chapter 14: When Networking and Prospecting, Use Your Contacts ... 4
Chapter 15: Develop new behaviors/ Love being better than you were yesterday 4
Chapter 16: Remember that 4
Chapter 17: Motivate, Motivate, Motivate 4
Chapter 18: Dream and believe in Possibilities 4
Chapter 19: Integrity: Keep your Word and do what you said 4
Chapter 20: Stop the Whining and Start the Winning 4
Chapter 21: Be Grateful 4
Chapter 22: We do live in a Galaxy, in a Universe 4
About author 4
Acknowledgements 1

SALES SUCCESS FOR THE ROOKIE

How to Succeed at Sales Right from the Start

STEPHEN P. LENTINI

ACKNOWLEDGEMENTS

First and foremost I thank God for every blessing and in fact every moment of my life…for all of my gifts and talents and I strive every day to use them to the fullest…giving God all the praise and glory.

I want to thank Justin Sachs, President of Motivational Press, and all of the Motivational Press staff that I have worked with…everyone reflects the attitude of "service" and all have done a great job and cheerfully.

This book would not be in your hands without Justin and his capable crew…thank you, thank you, thank you!

I want to thank Toni Stone who inspired me to keep going, who, edited the first edition and helped me with chapter titles and so many things. She taught me to say "thank you" when life says "hooray" and to say "thank you" when life is not cheering you on, after-all, everything is just a perspective.

And to my children, Beth, Lisa and Paul, My Son in Laws, Greg and Neil…you are my best work on this planet and I am so very grateful for what each of you bring to my life. Teagan and Logan and Taylor, my grandchildren again, my cheerleading squad.

I want to say thank you to Kathyann, To Melissa, Ashley, Chris, Thomas, Ma, my granddaughters, Lacey and Lauren.

To all of the students and clients who are the reason I do what I do, thank you.

To my family, who helped shape me, especially Frank, who inspired me to sell…..and to Dave, who has since left this world, who taught me the power of no and how to live "independent of the good opinion of others and to all my brothers and my sister Lorraine who always helps and inspires me. To Stan, my twin……thanks for always showing me…..well…me. And Seb, my oldest brother still to this day is an shining example of keep going no matter what.

To my Mother Rose and Dad, who showed me what perseverance meant. They raised seven children and always did the right thing. For Rose, integrity was key.

To my friend and business partner, John Smith, MJ, his wife. We have shared much and so very memorable. So much more to go and I am very grateful we met and for all you do and have done for me.

To Warren Gibbons, Paolo Scoglio, Mary Franklin and Nancy Chisholm, who helped teach my classes and kept me grounded.

To Jeff Ferreira, Jim Kaloutas, Jim Robbins, Sue DiiOrio, Rich DiiOrio, Pat Tormey, Joe Waldbaum and Dave Gilman, your friendship and success is an inspiration.

To my friends, Phil Albright, Ron Loto, Maggie Lohnes, GaryBrustas, George Leon, Jodi Knight, Peter Panagakos, John and Pat Calvert (Pat I know you are watching from heaven) and Paul Dimanno, also now watching from heaven, being able to speak to you anytime is a real gift, you are all blessings in my life.

To Gifford, Tod, Rich, Tim, Wendy, Robin, Deb, Michelle, Tracy and Steve Overton, Tadd and Julie, Christopher, Alex……thanks for helping me stay grounded and for knocking off my crown every so often.

To Michael Swaidner of POP Color Printing who made this first editions a reality.

To Mike Palechek, Thank you all, your support and referrals have been instrumental in my success…..

To Marc Borak and all the folks at Borax Paper, Eric Steen, and the Infusytems team, David Hirsch, Cindy Ciaccio, Sid Lerman and all the folks at Weeks Lerman, Steven and Larry Stern and all the folks at Supreme Industrial you all had a positive impact on my life and contributed greatly to getting me started on my path ….of independent consultant, speaker and trainer

I am so very blessed and grateful to have you all in my life.

Thanks Doll

Regards, Steve

FOREWORD 1
A FEW THOUGHTS TO PREPARE THE GROUND

When I met Steve, I was 29 years young and I had been selling software to pharmaceutical customers for almost 6 years. Early on, I had been very successful in my career and I had mentors that helped me learn the 'basics' of selling.

However, in the two years before I met Steve, I had switched companies two times and I was probably 6 months away from leaving sales altogether. I was struggling with my own identity as a salesperson and everything was an effort. I was having trouble with my interactions with colleagues and management.

In my very first discussion with Steve (now almost 11 years ago), Steve taught me that If you move towards the 'uncomfortable", things will change, you will change. He said that you should not expect a different result if you continue doing things the same way you always have. I am glad I listened.

Are you ready to get uncomfortable?

In a recent conversation with Steve, he reminded me that the idea of being comfortable in your life/career has changed dramatically in the past 20 years. As we look at the world around us, we see people gravitate to alcohol or drugs to seek out comfort. In order to be successful, we must live in the world of being "uncomfortable", we must not fear saying how we feel, we should not fear change.

Steve bestows gratitude on everything that comes. Even when the world seems to be working against me, he helps me to see the lesson in it. He has helped me acknowledge how I feel, and not simply react to stimuli. Instead I have learned to address how I feel and find a way to say it. This has helped me interact with customers, my colleagues, and even my in-laws. When I am with a customer, I have prepared for our meeting, I stay fully present, I observe, I listen, and when the time comes, I say what I feel.

To do this effectively, I had to learn how to say what I feel, and I have to get uncomfortable.

Many sales training programs may help you learn how to deal with situations that come up, but true life rarely mimics these situations. Also, our customers are smarter than that…they don't want to hear script, they want to buy from a real person.

Steve has taught me how to say what needs to be said, what I <u>feel</u>, without it being 'scripted'. Steve was a Sandler trainer and he learned a lot about what it takes to be a good salesperson but Steve's sales training is not a 'role play'. It can be applied to any customer, any experience. By learning how to listen to your customer, not being afraid of the uncomfortable, place gratitude on what comes, <u>you change.</u> Only then, can you help your customer, and your company, be successful. Ultimately, though, Steve has changed me, not just the salesperson or sales manager. He has changed the person I am.

My thoughts and words have power

I realized that I was blaming others for my current situation. I blamed the company's management for not being customer-centric and I made wild accusations about their motivations. I had completely taken on the victim role and hadn't recognized how I had created my situation and how I needed to change. Everything I thought had power, my words had power, and I was not powerless. I can now recognize these thoughts when they come up… Even though negative thoughts can find their way in, I can recognize them, bless them…and send them away. I am not perfect, and my words may sometimes reflect this, but because of Steve's teaching, I can hear myself now.

I can even help to recognize when others are living in a victim state of being. In some cases, I can try to help them see this. And other times, I just bless them for being there, reminding me….

How can I expect to receive, if I can't give?

Steve teaches that you will not see wealth if you hold onto money. He teaches us that we should be grateful for what is bestowed upon us and we should show this by giving. He practices what he preaches.

When we first started to work together, Steve and I met for lunch. I watched him give the cashier a large tip and I commented that I would never do that.

Steve challenged me to give away something that meant a lot to me. It was this 'project' that led me on a path of self-discovery.

I owned a BMW 325i that was only a few years old. My husband and I were expecting our first child and so we purchased an SUV. We were planning to sell the car and had gotten an offer of $16,000 for the vehicle. This would have been a nice amount of money and I had intended to use it to pay bills, etc. when I was out of work on maternity leave.

When Steve asked what I was going to give away, I knew the answer. I needed to give away the BMW. I had a family member that was having car issues and I knew this would be a blessing for her. This was difficult for me, but easy for my husband. I always knew he was more giving than me, but this was proof.

This project was necessary for me to grow, to let go, and to become the type of person I am today. I gave the car away and never accepted a dollar from her. A few months later, I closed the largest sale in the company's history to a biotechnology company and the commission check was for $16,000! The world works in mysterious ways....

Be grateful for all of it

I don't always show gratitude. I don't always have blessings for the negative aspects of my life, but I know that when I do, these 'misgivings' help me shape the person I want to be.

I recently had a call with Steve where I was telling him that my manager was rescheduling our 1:1 calls and not being very interactive or responsive. I fell into being a victim, feeling like I was under-valued. Steve was able to quickly help me see the positives in this behavior. My manager's lack of micromanagement was actually helping me be self-sufficient. Steve pointed out where my recommendations had been accepted (thus valued) and that I was able to make many connections within my large company because my manager was letting me figure it out myself. It was only this conversation that helped me move out of being a victim of the circumstance, and, instead, see how this current working environment was beneficial to my development as a manager. I became grateful for him in a way I would never have done before. I looked for ways to support my manager, and he accepted my ideas for changes within our sales organization.

Find a way to say how you feel

Steve has helped me find strategies for saying what I feel. Depending on the situation and the customer personality, there are different approaches that work. Again, this isn't role play, this is just something that comes natural to Steve and he has been able to help me say what I feel and it has changed things for me.

Set goals and visualize the results

In 2007, I had just started with my current company and I had been challenged by Steve to list my personal and professional goals. I had written down my current prospects and put measurable goals for each. Steve challenged every one of these goals. He also asked me *visualize* how this would be achieved. He asked me to see the PO in my hand. He asked me to try to feel the paper...and feel my emotions...how would I feel when my customer said yes? I did what he asked. The customer that I wrote down on that paper on May 7 2007 became the company's first ever $5M customer on December 17 2007.

I now have proof that there is POWER in writing down my goals and use these goals to guide my thoughts. There is so much power in this. I challenge you to try it!

And, when I find myself "hiding out" and not doing what I should, Steve has helped me to be able to recognize it and get back on track.

In closing, working with Steve has helped me see that sometimes things may look messy and unclear and that's ok. I am now well-trained to not judge anything by the way it looks in the moment, I judge things by my intention for the outcome. It would be silly for a farmer to scream at the seed in the ground upon planting it and expect an instant tomato. There is a process that happens in life, and we cannot always control exactly what it looks like.

What we CAN control is how we THINK about the process and I promise you that reading Steve's book will help you with that, more than you can imagine...enjoy.

Sue DiIorio, Director of Sales
Bioinformatics Software

FOREWORD 2
GET READY TO CHANGE

When I was asked to contribute to Steve's new book, I was both honored and excited. I have spent the last 20 years in medical sales and have been through numerous sales and coaching seminars. Without question, my experiences working with Steve Lentini have been the most impactful on both a personal and professional level. The ability for Steve's wisdom to reach the masses is a tremendous opportunity for those that wish sharpen their selling skills.

 I first came to know Steve through my wife who has spent many years working with him as her sales coach and mentor. After seeing her immeasurable professional success as a sales rep and sales leader, I decided to enlist Steve's help for my own sales organization. I invited Steve to speak at our national sales meeting to the team of experienced medical device sales representatives. After having been through countless presentations, with mixed results, we were struck by his simple yet powerful message…"be in the moment". Two years later, I still have members of my team talk about how "being in the moment" during their sales calls has allowed them to have a more consultative sales approach. Steve had a unique way of delivering the message that few have the ability to pull off. He was able to have the team "feel" what they needed to do and not just hear it and forget it by the end of the week. That, to me, is the sign of someone that is a true coach.

 We have had Steve continue to work with three of our high potential sales reps. They all have been identified as the next in line to become part of the sales leadership team. It was certainly going to be a challenge to work with three different reps, with three different skill sets, and three completely different backgrounds. A cookie cutter approach that I see way to often in selling seminars and coaching would never be successful. Steve was able to tailor his work based on specific needs and, in less than a year, the results were transformational. All three have taken huge strides in their professional career and have been promoted since taking part in the program. One of the best comments I have heard is "I am in the best professional shape of my life and Steve is the reason".

I am truly excited for Steve to publish this book for a couple of reasons. Firstly, he deserves every bit of success after what he has been able to accomplish for countless people both personally and professionally. Secondly, if you're willing to learn from Steve and are open to improving your selling skills and perfecting your craft, then reading this book will undoubtedly be a huge step in realizing your full potential.

For years working with Steve directly has been the only opportunity to tap into his knowledge and abilities. "Sales Success for Rookies" will be an opportunity for this knowledge to be spread to anyone who is willing to take the time to improve.

If you are reading this book, congratulations, you are about to become a significantly better sales rep. I know every member of team, regardless of experience and expertise, will read it.

Good Selling!

Richard A. DiIorio
Vice President of Sales
Boston, MA

Section 1
Seeds of the Sale

PREFACE

This book is about getting started in sales and succeeding right from the start. It's about learning how to help prospects buy versus selling. You will not have to "push to get the sale", which mostly pushes prospects away. You can be yourself and learn how to "say what you are feeling". You can sell the truth. You will not have to learn any tactics. "Tactics are tacky." Selling is about being in relationship. People buy from people they like and trust. If you sell with integrity and you sell your truth, people will like and trust you. You will attract what you require in life. Who wouldn't recommend or buy from someone whose reputation is one of integrity, whose main interest is in serving their higher calling by working to serve those that they sell to? Who wouldn't see the value in someone who would walk away from a sale because they see that the solution or conditions are not a good fit for either of them in the long term?

Learning to sell from integrity means listening for what would best serve the customer and not our next bonus or commission. It means living true to our higher calling, listening to our soul, and doing what, "in integrity", is the best for all concerned.

In this book, you will learn how to gain the respect and admiration of your customers and prospects by letting your true and real self shine. You can be yourself in sales if you learn which behaviors to control and which behaviors to emphasize on a sales call and in any relationship in life. You can let go of worry over quotas, and you can stop trying to manipulate others with the "next clever thing to say". There's no need to sell anything if you are listening for what would solve your customer's or prospect's problems. If you are listening to see if they are a good fit for your company, and you are willing to let them go, either to another solution or to a competitor who is a better fit, prospects will buy.

You will learn how to relax and let your customer sell himself. -You will learn how to walk him to that sale. You will learn to stop doing business with people who don't respect you, and instead command respect and sell more.

Selling should be fun and what's more fun than being in control of your life, your destiny and yourself. After all, the only thing you can control is you and that's what this book will focus on. As you change, things change. I often say, "If you don't like your experience of the world, change how the world is experiencing you."

Learning how to communicate to improve your sales is one path to take. Improved communication by itself is not enough. Learning what has been holding you back is the key. I managed salespeople for many years, over 30 in fact, and I have conducted sales training courses for over 12 years. The one thing that I observed over and over was that, even salespeople that had great communication skills, "hit the wall" and fell short of their goals. The reason-- they focused on things outside of themselves to fix the problem when they were the problem. The great motivational speaker and author, Jim Rohn, once said, "The harder I worked on myself, the better my business did."

In this book, you will learn how to begin the journey of working on your "self". How to take your "self" on. That is what I teach in all of my classes. Training on better ways to sell is a positive thing. Training yourself to see your "default patterns" will add more happiness, joy, fulfillment and money than sales training alone, in the long run.

Adding a "Higher Power" to your life is a necessary component as well. Remember, we do live in a galaxy, in a Universe. You can honor your higher calling through your work. You can bring your soul with you to work. In this book, you will learn how to add a "spiritual power" and enlightened way of thinking that will provide an ease and satisfaction to your work. If practiced, you will find joy and satisfaction, while you reach your goals. You will also learn to understand and plan using the "seasons"; just like nature has seasons, there are seasons in sales. You will learn about the Universal Laws of Success. Studied by many successful people, I build upon the work by Napoleon Hill, Wayne Dyer, Deepak Chopra, Jim Rohn and many others who have written about the Laws of Success.

"Selling can be fun and easy when *you go with the flow."*

"Going with the flow" is a new concept to grasp in sales. The words, "going with the flow" invoke an uncomfortable feeling in most type "A" sales people. They believe that everything happens in response to some action that they take. They have the attitude of "always be closing". They feel it is necessary to keep the "pressure on" by having the next greatest thing to say that will close the prospect. Prospects who have been properly helped to buy won't have to be closed. Don't get me wrong, action in sales is a necessary thing and many good results come from action. Albert Einstein once said "nothing happens until something moves". "Going with the flow" doesn't imply, not to take action. What I mean by saying "go with the flow", is developing an intuitive sense of what to do next. Going with the flow is paying attention to how you "feel" during a sales call or in any situation, and finding a way to say what you are "feeling," Dave Sandler of Sandler Sales

Institute always said, "If you feel it, find a way to say it." I say, "Always sell the truth, and if the truth won't sell, don't sell it."

TIP:
If you have to lie to make a sale, don't.

You can sense what the necessary next steps are by paying attention to both how the conversation is going, and a prospect's body language, tone and expressions. You are helping the prospect or customer by allowing them space to have their feelings and opinions, and in return, the prospect builds a stronger sense of trust and comfort with you. Sales increase and customer bonds are stronger and longer lasting if you can learn to "go with the flow".

I learned selling with integrity by always being honest, and noticing how prospects responded so enthusiastically to me; if they did not buy that day, often they did buy or call me later. Many times, prospects have called after the company they previously did business with showed them a lack of integrity. I also learned by having a lack of integrity in my personal life, that it cost me. I was able to "wake up" and notice the difference in my integrity with clients and customers and how it served me well to serve them well. Applying the laws of integrity in all aspects of my life has had amazing benefits. When I changed, things changed. The common denominator, in all of my life situations, was me.

I've worked with many sales people over the years, and have witnessed things that made their job so much more difficult. The main reason for their difficulty was that they never shut up long enough to listen to their customers. Their customers were telling them the secret to selling them. Some of these "so-called salespeople" loved hearing themselves so much that they never stopped talking long enough to observe great salespeople at work, and they never absorbed another way of doing things. In fact, they thought they were so great, they never asked successful people what it was that they could do to be more successful. So, here it is - if you want it - all the information you'll ever need to keep selling with integrity.

CHAPTER 1: STAY CERTAIN OF SUCCESS

Think positive thoughts about yourself and the prospect. Do you remember a time when you sensed a friend, spouse, co-worker or your child seemed down or blue? Can you tell when someone has a great attitude? Is really enthused about something? We can all sense how others around us are feeling and this goes for your prospects as well. They can sense the same about you. The entire universe is energy. Your thoughts are energy. Project only the best energy by disciplining your thoughts before you go into a sales call. I salute the "Divinity" within all of the people that I meet each day. I am always thinking and disciplining my thoughts. In fact, practice disciplining your thoughts at all times and it will be second nature in a sales call. The side benefit will be that the world around you will change as you change your thinking. *Earl Nightingale said "you become what you think about."*

Notice now, what is it that dominates your thoughts all day long? Napoleon Hill, in *Think and Grow Rich*, suggests writing out what you desire with a designated time frame that you will accomplish it by, add what you will *give, (giving is key to receiving in life) and what you intend to do with your desire. Read it every morning and evening, when you get up and before you go to bed.* I personally use this method, along with visualization, meditation and affirmations every day. All of these ingredients have added immense success to my life along with joy and satisfaction.

Regardless of how you are feeling, *act as if* you are confident. Change your body language to reflect how a confident person would carry themselves; walk like a confident person would walk. By *acting as if* you are confident, you will notice that in a short time you will feel confident. Those around you will sense that confidence.

If you have a belief in a "Higher Power", the Divine or God, you can bring a miracle power-- into your sales call, your work day -- that "nothing (no thing) is out of order in the Universe..." *Steve Lentini.* And that is so in your life. Spend some time each day in silence and listen to what your soul is telling you. "The Master is within, life is the teacher." *Steve Lentini.* Pay attention to your inner self. Follow those intuitions.. Wayne Dyer says, "everything in the Universe came from nowhere, now here." Follow those prompts. Pay attention to the results of following those prompts. I use a journal to record what happens when I follow my intuition -- those thoughts that come from nowhere. Prove to yourself that intuition is guidance from your Higher Self, the Universal energy, your soul, whatever you choose to call it -- prove it.

TIP:

You are what you think about. Notice your predominant thought patterns.

Even if you do not believe in a Higher Power, nothing is out of order anyway. How could it be? How would earth remain suspended in the midst of darkness, with all that is required for life right here and now, if anything was out of order? There is something that is keeping the planets orbiting in perfect order, keeping the Universe from flying apart. As Deepak Chopra says in his book *Power, Freedom and Grace*, "When you have a conscious awareness of your soul, you experience everything as a miracle."

Remember, when you feel that things are out of control, to surrender to the idea that things are happening as they should. As Eckert Tolle says in his book *The Power of Now*, "there is only now." When you accept the moment, you create space for something new, perhaps a miracle to appear. Eckert also says, "when you fight life, life fights you."

Pay attention to what you can do that is in your control. You cannot control others, so release them. You focus on you. The serenity prayer says, "God, grant me the serenity to accept the things I cannot change, the courage to change the things I can and the wisdom to know the difference." If you are willing to surrender to what is and focus only on what you can change, you are left with the energy to work with all your gifts and talents. You will be happy because, knowing that you have done your best, you let the rest go. You will be amazed at the dimension of joy that is added to your life as a result. People around you will notice your peaceful demeanor. Clients and prospects will notice as well, and bringing this kind of thinking to your work will positively affect your results.

Thoughts are things. Lynne McTaggert, in her book *The Intention Experiment* says, "Dozens of scientists have produced thousands of papers in the scientific literature offering sound evidence that thought is capable of profoundly affecting all aspects of our lives." As observers and creators, we are constantly remaking our world at every instant. Every thought we have, every judgment we hold, however unconscious, is having an effect. With every moment that it notices, the conscious mind is sending an intention. Pay attention to your thoughts. Forward your aim to your desired result, intend its outcome. Visualize the outcome and feel what it will feel like to get it -- see the rewards, see the happy clients faces, see the $$$$$ that will come your way.

Notice too, what has been your predominant thought pattern, and does it match what you are currently harvesting in your life? Without even knowing you, I would say without a doubt the answer is yes. Otherwise, who is creating this result? Are you a circumstance in your life or the creator of your experience? The choice is yours and your world will form around that choice.

I prefer to be the creator and not the circumstance. Think about it and make the conscious choice from today forward to intend what you want to create and to create from what you intend. Do not let anything deter you. When thoughts of doubt appear, send them packing. When others who doubt your choices appear (and they will, they are after all reflections of your own doubt), send them packing as well.

My teacher, Toni Stone says, "Remember too, that things will not appear to be as you want them, until they are." This is the argument for perseverance. Stick with it no matter what.

Even if you do not believe in God or an Infinite Intelligence, if you are an atheist, you can bring "positive energy" and positive thoughts with you on your sales calls and at all times. The Universe is teeming with energy -- you are energy and your thoughts have energy. How is it that on the phone someone else can detect if we are feeling down? Or perhaps you have noticed that when you have called someone that they are agitated or depressed. How is it that you noticed? You heard it in their voice. Your energy level can be detected in person and on the phone. Bring positive thoughts and the great energy associated with positive thinking with you in every moment and watch your success skyrocket.

CHAPTER 2: ASK THEM WHAT THEIR NEEDS ARE AND MAKE A PURCHASE HAPPEN

You do not want everyone as a customer; you only want "good" customers. Good customers make a good company - and a good commission. The only way to determine which of the many prospects you want for customers is to let them tell you about their company and needs; they can't do this if you are doing the talking. You'll have plenty of time to tell them all about your company later. Prepare questions before the call that will help you get useful information and allow you to match good prospects with your company's strengths. Remember Who, What, Where, When, Why and How? Some examples are: "What do you look for in a supplier?" "What issues or challenges are you facing in your business that you see us helping you with?" "Of those things that you just shared, which is most important?" "Which is least important?"

If they tell you about any issues with one of their suppliers, some other great questions to ask are:

"How long have you been dealing with this?" (If they answer this with "Oh, a long, long time", it probably means that they are not motivated to fix the problem). "What if we fixed 85% of the issue?" "What if we could only fix 50% of the issue?" "How would you fix the issue?" These questions help you understand if the prospect has realistic expectations about solving the problem.

Use past, present, future, as suggested by author and sales trainer, Steve Schiffman. "Please give me some history on this issue, what were your biggest challenges in the past? Today, any issues? And now? What about going forward? How do you see the future if you do not fix this now? In the past, how have you addressed these issues? Presently, how are you dealing with this? For you, with this issue, what is the ideal future solution?" Other good questions are "What are some of your goals for the company / department this year?" "How could we help you achieve those goals?"

Take notes, listen, and look for gestures and expressions of emotion on these answers. If there are none, perhaps they are just shopping. You could ask, "I could be wrong, but I sense there is no real urgency to deal with this issue just now, is that correct?"

TIP: You could say "no" too; remember, not everyone is a fit.

If you see or feel a lot of emotion with some of the responses, you could say, "I noticed that you were really expressive when I asked xxxxxx... would you tell me more about that?" The emotion indicates that you have struck a nerve, a real issue for him or her; if you have the best solution here, you are on the way to making the sale. Keep asking questions and listen to what they would do to fix it, and then ask, "What if I had 80% of that solution?" Again, listen; then you could ask, "What is your budget to fix the problem?" Make sure here that they are realistic about the investment to fix the problem and that it fits your pricing structure.

Understanding what makes your prospect special in the marketplace or in their eyes could be important to determining if you can help this prospect, so ask questions like "What separates you from your competition?" or "where are you planning to take the company in the marketplace?"

Also, the right questions, tactfully asked, such as "How many deliveries do you require?" and "What's your company's average time frame for invoice payment?" will help you structure viable business deals for good customers and discourage frustrating habits such as late payments, small orders, last minute deliveries, etc. Use the Covey method. *Stephen Covey suggests, "In anything that we want to achieve, start with the end in mind."* Whatever industry you are in or service you provide, start with what is the ideal prospect or customer for you. Then create the questions that would provide you with the information to determine if the interview is going your way.

You have the right to determine if prospects are really committed to changing.

TIP:

Help people buy; selling is dead.

Owning this information also allows you to walk away from customers that have no business acumen. Remember to listen carefully to the answers and don't hesitate to take notes. If you can't recall the answers when you need them, why ask?

The most important part of selling, is to keep your focus on the prospect or customer. When others are doing the talking we are most likely to learn how to sell someone or what they would buy.

If you are asking questions, the prospect is speaking; your job is to get information, not to give it. The prospect should be talking 60 – 75% of the time. If they are, fine, you are doing your job. If not, and you notice that you are doing most of the talking, stop; then start asking the questions. If you have prepared before the call, thinking about what you would like to know about the prospect, you learn to follow a system on a sales call, and your success ratio will improve. Following a system will help you stay on track. I will help you develop a system later in this book.

RELATIONSHIP SKILLS ARE KEY

Doing business is a relationship, and relationships are defined between two or more people. Certainly, you will have people that you will not want to do business with. The only way to determine which prospects you want for customers is to let them tell you about their company and their needs.

Also use questions to help you achieve more in life and reach your goals -- ask for help.

Everything that we require in this life comes from someone else. Asking is the key to getting what we want. Many of us feel that if we are not working hard, we are not really doing anything worthwhile or that "things just do not come easy to us." That is how I used to feel. Working hard distracted me from dealing with my real feelings. Working hard is how I used to determine my self-worth. I would never ask anyone for help because it was a sign of weakness. It meant that I had to admit that this (whatever it was) project or problem was something that I could not do or solve myself. I now realize how this kind of thinking held me back. I changed my mind and thinking about asking for help. I could ask for the order and not for help. *I ask for help all the time now. I ask for referrals, for ideas and suggestions on how they would grow the business if they were me, for help with a new contact, etc.*

My life has changed significantly for the better. People love to help. I was always willing to help others and did help many people, yet I was unwilling to ask for help for myself. I remember refusing help offered by others who obviously could see that I was struggling with something. Besides asking questions of prospects and customers to help you sell easily, remember to ask for help with achieving your goals and daily tasks.

Oh, and by the way, don't forget to ask for the business. Use a thermometer to take the temperature of your prospects. Ask, "on a scale of 1 to 10, if 1 was you were not convinced that we had the solution to your problem and 10 was you would move to the next step, where are you on that scale?" If the answer is five, six or seven, ask "what would you need to hear to get to an 10?" Listen very intently here, because they are going to tell you how to get the order. You can then say "What if I could get you 85% of that?" (under promise and over deliver, you can always give them 90% or more of what they want and pleasantly surprise them). "What would happen next?" Again, listen intently, you might hear something like, "Well, if you could do that, when would you start?" (buying signal). Listen for buying signals.

On the other hand, if the answer to your "on a scale of 1 to 10" question you hear a "one, two, three or four", do not panic, (after all, you can't lose what you don't have), you could say, " Well, I must have missed something, is there anything that I could say that would get you to a five?" Again, listen intently. You could also say, "Well, I must have missed something, do you mind if I review with you what you just told me about the issue?" And then go over your notes. Confirm what they told you and ask what you are missing. If it is "no", fine. Ask what you could have done better before you go. At least get a lesson if you cannot get the order. Ask also, "Do you mind if I check in with you from time to time?" If you have made them comfortable, perhaps they will buy from you in the future.

Ask and prepare questions, starting with the end in mind from now on, and follow it. You will be amazed at the results.

TIP:
"You can help them make a purchase, the best purchase for them, and that is being in integrity."

When it's your turn to speak, and it will be your turn at some point, address only the needs or concerns that they shared with you. If you have questioned and listened well, you will know by now if your product or service is a fit for your prospect. Help your prospects make the proper buying decision. If the truth won't sell, don't sell it. Product knowledge is wonderful, but save it until after you've gotten enough information about filling a need or solving a problem. Jeffrey Gittomer says in his book titled *The Little Red Book of Selling*, "They don't want your sales pitch. They want answers to their situations and concerns."

If your product or service will not answer their concerns or address their needs, then tell them. Educate them on what your strengths are and let them decide if they would like to continue at this point. You could say, "We're not the best at addressing x, although we are, as our customers tell us, very good at y. What should we do now? Should we continue?" If they say yes, you could ask, "Gee, if we're not a really good fit for x, then I'm curious, why would you like to hear about y?"

It important here that you are really feeling curious, I know that I would be. If you feel something, find a way to say it. Listen intently and take notes on their answer, your honesty paves the way for a better relationship and provides a way for the prospect to trust you. If you cannot help them now, believe me, they will be glad to invite you in later when other opportunities arise. Prospects will also stretch their current opportunity to match your strengths where feasible because of the trust you are building by selling honesty.

That's why I say, if the truth won't sell, don't sell it.

TIP: Be authentic, forget commissions and sell solutions to problems, even if the solution is not yours.

CHAPTER 3: BE UPFRONT AND GO FOR NO

How many sales people are comfortable going for *no*? We worry about rejection. We cannot relax. Starting at *no* is more fun and it takes the pressure off of both of you.

TIP: You cannot lose what you do not have.

Instead of going for *no* early, we let the customer have control of the sale and we waste time and resources in calls that are going nowhere. We wait and wonder if the customer finds value in what we say.

Let me suggest a different approach. Give your customer/prospect the opportunity to say *no* and watch what happens. I guarantee that 70 - 80% of the time that the real dialogue will begin after the first *no*.

Here is an example of giving your customer or prospect the opportunity to say *no* –

"Thank you Mr. / Ms. Prospect for inviting me in. I have prepared an agenda for our time together. Do you mind if I review it? I'm going to ask you some questions about your company and then you can ask me about mine. If after our exchange you cannot see a reason for our two companies to get together for now, for this moment, would you mind sharing that with me? I am okay with it. If, on the other hand, you do see a reason to move forward, would you let me know that as well? Then together we can determine what the next step will be. Are you okay with that?"

Giving your prospect the opportunity to say *no* is refreshing. A sales person who is trying to take the pressure off of them will surprise them.

If they say *no*, ask them why? Listen carefully. Your true selling starts here.

TIP:

No is a sales person's friend, relax at no, go with it and find GOLD!

For example, if after your questions you ask, "Well Mr. /Ms. Prospect, have you heard or seen any reason for me to continue?" If they respond, "no", now ask, "May I ask why?" Let's suppose the prospect responds, "Well, I'm happy with my current supplier and I'm not going to change." You could respond, "I appreciate that; under what circumstances would you consider a change?" <u>Listen</u> - or you might say, "I hear that you are happy with your current supplier, however, no one is perfect. In fact, we're not; but if you had a magic wand, what, if anything, would you improve about your current supplier?"

Do you see what I am saying? Even after you get a *no*, you have established dialogue after the *no*, with questions. It's the dialogue you want. Look for openings in their answers to your questions - listen carefully.

If it is really *no*, you have shortened the selling cycle, and now you can move on to more prospects sooner. Remember to remind them that *no* was for now. Ask if they mind if you return from time to time if you have an idea or suggestion for them. Ask them what kind of ideas or suggestions would they appreciate? What areas of their business are they looking for ideas to improve?

They will respect your approach and invite you back.

Whatever your concerns are, come up with a question that deals with the issue up front and wait for the answer. You will never need a "tacky tactic" if you say what you are feeling. Find a way to say it. If you feel uncomfortable about bringing something up, say that you feel uncomfortable about something and you wondered if you could bring up something that they might find uncomfortable.

Whatever your fears are, find a way to bring them up as well. If someone asks for your pricing early in the sales call, you might fear that they are just shopping to compare and give your pricing to their current supplier. If you feel that, you would say, "My biggest fear is that if I give you a price list now, you will bring it to your current supplier just to lower your pricing. I have had that happen before. Could it be the reason you are asking for pricing just now?"

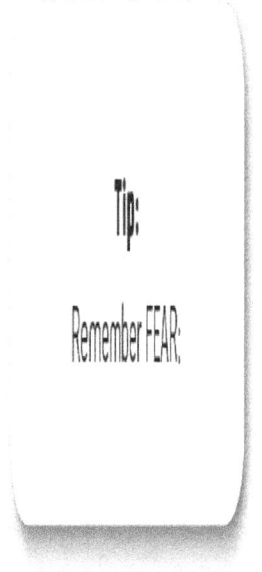

Tip:

Remember FEAR.

Remember my acronym for FEAR: Facing "Enormous" Adversity Realistically/Responsibly. When we feel fear, it is an indicator from our body that some action is required on our part. Face it. Walk into it. I put the word "Enormous" in quotes because often when we fear something, we have made it enormous. When we get to the other side of the issue, we look back and think, "Why did I fear that? It was not a big deal after all". I say realistically/responsibly as some situations call for common sense. If your personal safety is involved for example, *realistically* would mean get out of there. *Responsibly* would mean to be sure that our response is with integrity, that we do the right thing.

FACING "ENORMOUS" ADVERSITY REALISTICALLY/RESPONSIBLY

If you notice that something you said may have upset the prospect, bring it up. You could say, I'm feeling like I have said something that upset you, is that the case?

If the prospect says something that confuses you or says something that you are curious about, find a way to say it.

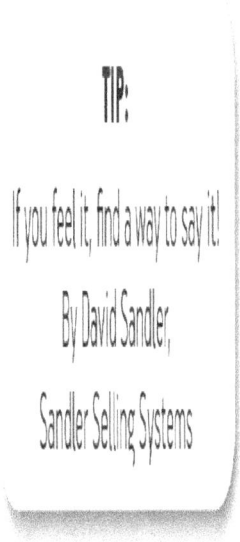

TIP:
If you feel it, find a way to say it!
By David Sandler,
Sandler Selling Systems

Whatever you feel, if you trust in your gut and find a way to say what you are feeling, your sales will increase as you get into the real dialogue that the answers to these types of questions will bring.

This is called the "Pendulum Theory of Communication", to have an adult-adult conversation, your goal is to always stay farther on the negative (Not OK) than the positive (OK).

Most prospects will be refreshed with your honesty and find a way to help you keep the sale.

There is nothing to remember in this selling method, just be yourself, be honest and if you feel it, use that.

In communication, your goal is always to have an adult-adult conversation. That is achieved by always saying what you feel. Soften with soft people and hit the tough people with it hard, mirroring each of them. Tough people like and respect tough people. The same goes for softer style folks. Just mirror them. Take a look at the diagram below:

Take a look at each position on the pendulum.

12: No/Never buy, abrupt.

11: Takes phone calls when you are there, obnoxious,

Don't want you here, rude

10: Defending competition

9: Shuts you off

8: Fidgeting, inattentive, and occasionally listening
7: Uncomfortable
6: Neutral
5: Maybe, head nods, wishy-washy
4: Sounds good
3: Likes you
2: Enthusiastic
1: Sold/Yes

Where ever your prospect is on the pendulum, you stay on the negative side. If they are sold, #1, you drop down to #4, by saying "Sounds good, tell me what you mean by "wow, I've been wanting to get that from you?" A good many sold or enthusiastic prospects either have no money or no intention of ever buying. They are people pleasers who cannot say "no" to your face. These are the people that you chase with voice mails, after they tell you, "Oh, yes, I'll get it on Monday, just call me then". On the other end of the scale, say at #12, they say, "No not today, not ever from your company", you would say, "You sound upset with us, what happened, tell me about it?" You would also be saying what you feel at this moment. Instead of defending your company, be empathetic and be curious about what happened. Give the upset person the space for their feelings and let them vent. Don't apologize until you have heard the whole story. Agree with them if you can, say, "Well, I'm not sure that I would buy from us after that." There is no guarantee that they will ever buy, but I have had some of the best sales in my life after a prospect or customer started with how angry they were with us and with "No, we'll never buy from you."

Be aware of where people start out on the pendulum of communication. Remember, your job in any sales conversation, especially if you have just met the prospect, is to stay below them, you stay "less ok" than they are if they are on the positive. And on the negative side, you would carefully mirror their negative, and use what I call a take away.

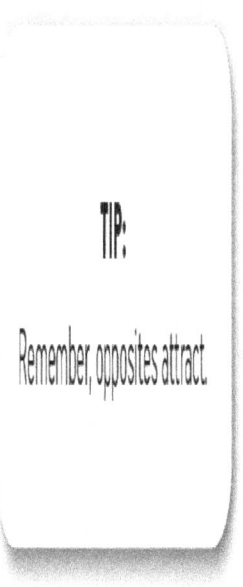

TIP:

Remember, opposites attract.

I once had a prospect come up to me at a cocktail reception and say "Oh, you're with XXXX, we could never buy from you." and I replied, "How do you know that we would sell you?" He was shocked that I might not want to sell them. I could see by his reaction. His spine stiffened. He asked, "How come you might not sell us?" I asked him, "Do you sell everyone?" He replied, "No." I asked, "Peter, (looking at his name badge) why not?" Peter replied, "Well, not everyone is a good prospect for us." I said, "Well, the reason we might not sell you is the same. You might not be a good fit for us. Tell me a little bit about why you said you would never buy from us." -- and that started a dialogue that ended with me closing his business a few weeks later; it was worth over $750,000 annually and I took the business from six other of his suppliers. He consolidated all of his purchases with me, despite doing business with some of those suppliers for many years -- in some cases for over ten years. Why did I close that business? I left him space for his opinions and I went more negative than he did on the pendulum of communication. The only way he could swing was more positive and he did.

TIP:

The Laws of Physics applies to communication, "a body in motion stays in motion", take a risk and keep the pendulum swinging.

CHAPTER 4: GIVE MORE BUT DON'T OVER PROMISE

The days of, "Yes, we can do it all" are over. Customers don't care about the size of your company, your warehouse, the number of trucks you have, how many employees, how many factories you have or any of the other things that may give your company bragging rights.

We are not measured by what we do right, but by how we deliver what we say. Do we keep our word and how do we correct issues and problems? Companies and people with integrity keep their word, no matter what.

What they want is for you to deliver what you promise. If you cannot keep all the promises you make, you are over promising and out of integrity. Leave yourself room by under promising, and then really impress customers by over delivering. Give yourself room to over deliver by asking, "When would you like this (completed/delivered)?" If the prospect's expectations are unreasonable, you could say, "What if I said it will be two weeks longer than that?" (you now have given yourself an additional week). If the prospect says, "That's ok," you have room to deliver *before* the two weeks are up. If the prospect stands firm on their original request and you know you cannot meet that date, you could say, "What would happen if we missed that date? How would you feel?" Let them talk. You want to help *them* hear that another week or two is not that critical and most times it's not. If it's still critical for the prospect to meet that delivery date and you cannot meet it, then you end it. You could say, "I want you to have the XXXX on time and I cannot promise that. Would you like me to refer another company or do you have one in mind?" Here, by allowing the prospect the space to go to a competitor and by offering to help them find another supplier, you build trust and respect that may reopen this door to a sale now or one in the future.

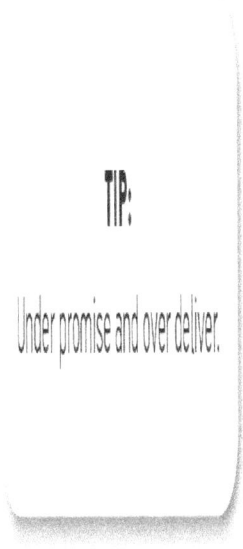

TIP:

Under promise and over deliver.

IF you are keeping your word everywhere in your life, then you have integrity. Notice if and when you break your word. Ask your significant other and friends if they see you as someone who keeps their word. They will tell you if you invite them to and share up front that it is better for you if they tell you the truth. You can only change, if you learn, what it is that you do not know about yourself.

There is what we know about ourselves, what we know that we don't know, and what we don't know that we don't know. I work with students and myself on learning "what I don't know, that I don't know." That is where true growth and continued success will manifest from.

CHAPTER 5: MAKE RELATIONSHIP, STAND IN THEIR SHOES AND GET TO KNOW THEM BETTER

If your first thought on every order or presentation is commission, you will see dollars shrink over time and have much slower growth in commission dollars than your counterparts who think "customers". By staying in the frame of mind that you are there to "help people buy the best solution, even if it's not you", you will grow your sales faster than those salespeople who focus only on their commissions. For your existing customers, do the little things: stay with them on an issue with another department in your company until it is resolved; fix annoying balances that linger on erroneous statements; make that return the customers keeps asking about; care enough to resolve issues that are "someone else's responsibility." Once someone becomes your customer, make them your responsibility, even if the company assigns another department to do the daily service. Take care of your customer's business and your commissions will grow, especially through referrals from happy customers. Jeffrey Gittomer, author of *The Little Red Book of Selling* says, "If you make a sale, you can earn a commission. If you make a friend, you can earn a fortune". Thinking "customer first, before commission," will take you to the bank more often.

"Get to know them better if you stand in their shoes"
Steve Lentini

You are first and foremost selling yourself. First impressions are the lasting ones. What is it that you want to portray to the prospects in the first few minutes? People buy from people they like and trust. Your job is to make the prospect comfortable with you. This is where bonding and appearance comes in. Let's start with the bond.

Bonding is one of the keys to sales. In my almost 30 years of coaching, managing, and training sales people, the biggest mistake they made was in the bond. Even though we hear about bonding all the time, many salespeople are unaware that it is how they show up that is their block to selling more. Remember, selling is about them, the prospect, not us.

  A. Match and mirror the prospect, stand in their shoes. Begin with body language first. Body language is 55% of the communication pie. Wait for the prospect to begin speaking and match their general posture. Do not play "Simon says" with the prospect. If the prospect is generally relaxed, match it. If they are sitting straight up, match it. This helps you because as you match someone, you get to feel what they are feeling in that same posture and it tells the other person's subconscious that you are like them. Your job is to help people find the right solution and to make them feel at ease with you as soon as possible. Who better to trust than someone who is helping them buy and who is more like them than not.

B. Match their tone and speed of their speech. If they talk soft and slow (usually together), match it. If they talk loud and fast, pick up your pace and volume. Tonality is 38% of the communication pie.

C. Match their need for bonding. This is most important. If you meet with someone and they want to get right to business and resist your attempts to bond, GET RIGHT TO BUSINESS. Be direct if they are direct. They will like that because it sends a message to their brain, "Hey, this person is just like me." Just follow the prospect's lead, go with the flow. For someone who wants to spend time with you on the bond, allot no more than 20% of the total time set aside for the appointment for the bond. Of a 60-minute call, allow for 12 minutes for bonding.

D. Thoughts have power. They are energy. Scientists have proven this. Think good thoughts. This sends good energy out from you. You can silently wish your prospect joy, success and happiness. Deepak Chopra, in his book the *Seven Spiritual Laws of Success*, says wishing someone "joy, success and happiness" is akin to bringing someone a gift who has invited you to their home. Hopefully, when invited to someone's home you would bring a gift, but Deepak says that if you did forget, this wish would be just like bringing them an actual gift. Imagine the power of doing this with your prospects.

E. Appearance is critical. Even though the work world has become more relaxed, appearance is critical for successful selling. As far as dress goes, dress professionally. Use common sense and remember the image you want to portray. Matching works here as well. Match the prospect's dress code. When you are setting the appointment ask, "What is the dress code at your office?"

What is your dress code saying to the prospect about you and your company? Sloppy dress, sloppy company? Sloppy dress says you have no confidence in your sales ability. The same goes for provocative dress. Dressed professionally, what does that say about you and your company? The same goes with personal hygiene. How do your teeth look? How about your hair? Do you have dandruff? I once coached a guy to wear light sport coats or light plaids to hide his skin condition. He was wearing blue and a dark sport coat and his shoulders and neck looked like a ski resort. You are the first contact with your company that any prospect has. Think about that before you go in.

F. Are you a person of integrity? Do you keep your commitments? Are you on time? Do you return phone calls in a timely fashion? Do you fulfill your promises? Trust is built on integrity. Keep your word everywhere and sell more. It will build trust and help you bond.

G. Forget about that old axiom, "look around the prospect's office to find something to bond about". You can use it if you wish, but prospects are aware of this tactic. Be yourself. I am curious about a person's background so I ask about their background in the company and sometimes I ask if they got recruited in. I'll say, "Tell me about your history in this company, did you get recruited in?" That is a subtle pat on the back, a stroke. People are stroke deprived. Most people in top-level management (I hope you are calling on top management) do not get enough strokes. If they were recruited, they usually tell me all about where they came from, and if not, I ask. If they started in the company mailroom or at the "bottom," they usually relish in telling me the history as well. It is what I am interested in and that is what I start with. I am naturally curious about people and their careers and how they succeed. Start with an interest of yours; be real, and be curious. If you do see a lot of paraphernalia around the office, ask about it, even if you are not a fan; if you are curious, ask. Remember, you do not need a "tacky tactic" if you are being real.

A word of caution though, I once noticed a lot of golf awards in the office of my prospect on a first visit. I said, "Wow, you sure are a great golfer -- three holes in ones?" He replied, "I can't stand golf." I said, "What about all the awards?" He replied, "It's not my office, we know salespeople use this stuff to try and bond so we switch offices here all the time when we have a salesperson come in for a first visit." Beware and ask first, "Is this your office?"

H. Once you ask that question, ("Tell me about your history in this company, did you get recruited in?"), watch what happens. People love to talk about themselves. After a while, with some follow up questions like, "What are your responsibilities?", you can return to selling by asking the prospect, "How can we help you with those responsibilities?"

I. Take notes. Ask permission first. Another stroke. May I take a few notes? Ask this after they have started sharing what is going on in the company. After you have gathered enough information about their situation, review what they have told you and validate it. It would sound like this. "May I review what you have just told me to be sure I have got it right?" Review and tell them, "This is typically what we are hearing from our customers" (validation by the way). Ask if you missed anything. Ask if they would like to add anything. Then ask, "How do you see an outside company helping you with these issues?" Listen closely, they will tell you how to sell them.

J. Take the pressure off. Tell them that you are there to help them find the right solution, even if it isn't you. Ask them if they are okay telling you that you are not the right fit for them. Tell them that you are okay with *no*. This is taking the pressure off of both of you. It is reminding you that that is why you are there, to see if it is a fit for both of you. Then you could say, "If I sense that your company is not a fit for us, would you mind if I say that?" After all, we do not sell everyone.

TIP: Make bonding a part of you, not a manipulative tactic. Practice being fully present in all your conversations.

CHAPTER 6: DETACH FROM OUTCOMES

Detaching from outcomes helps you relax in the middle of the action. How can you lose what you don't have? Being detached from outcomes, you can help people buy and be comfortable. Being detached will help you take risks with evasive buyers. How can you take a huge risk if you are attached and worried about not getting the sale?

*TIP:
Selling becomes easier when you go with the flow.

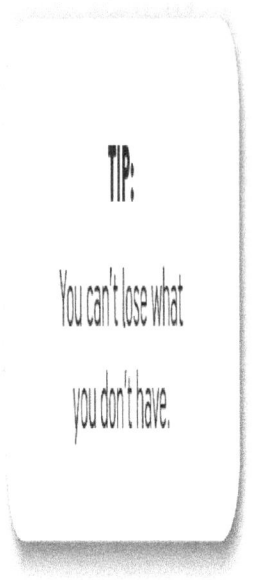

TIP: You can't lose what you don't have.

Remember, you don't have it. Take a risk. I spent many years attempting to control other people and thankfully realized what a waste of energy it was.

"After you learn to detach, relax and go with the flow, life works better everywhere"

Steve Lentini

Being detached from outcomes helps you with rejection. How can you be rejected, if you are not attached to the outcome? View everything as just an event, not good or bad, just outcomes. Since you cannot control outcomes in life, only yourself, focus on what you can control. YOU!

When you sense things aren't going where you wanted, don't push too hard, unless you are in front of a hard driving person. Let the customer know you can see that you've missed something, then ask directly: "What did I miss? How can we get back on track?" Watch for the telltale signs that you have upset someone. Notice body language. Is the prospect closing up? Is he/she moving away from you, pursing lips, furrowing their brow, or worse, crossing their arms and moving away from you at the same time? If there is anything that you sense, even a feeling that you have said something that upset them, find a way to say what you feel or see. Be prepared to soften the question first. People love to help people, so struggle on purpose if you have to. If you are feeling uncomfortable, share that. You could say, "I am feeling like you are upset, I could be wrong, tell me, are you uncomfortable with this purchase, or with me?" Give them a chance to respond. Whatever it is! It could even be, "Well, I get the sense that we are not a fit. Are you feeling the same way?"

TIP: Take a few deep breaths before or during the call to help you detach or just note your breathing.

Your goal is to help people buy. Some prospects buy because of force. They are tired of pestering. They do anything to get away from the constant barrage of phone calls and emails. These prospects do not stay customers for long. Often, they change their mind within 24 hours and cancel orders. Have you had, what you thought was an enthusiastic prospect, say that "things really looked good" and even after saying: "Call me on Monday and I'll give you an order," they still did not return your calls? It could be because you put too much pressure on them and you did not realize it. If this was the case, the prospect just wanted to be rid of you. They do not return calls. Do your research on this. Customers, given respect and the space to buy what fits, will stay your customers.

You waste energy pushing a customer who is a soft personality type, when they have decided it's a "no sale". It's your fault you missed something - use the energy instead to discover what you have missed or to move on to a new customer. Do the both of you a favor and voluntarily close a presentation that is going nowhere. Many times recognizing the ending actually opens real dialogue that might get a sale. So go with the flow. You are easier to be around and you will attract new outcomes.

The only exception to the above is when you are dealing with hard driving personality types. You must match and mirror them -- push them, prod them, give them back what they give you just as hard or harder -- they will like and respect you for it.

CHAPTER 7: DON'T SETTLE FOR LESS

Don't cave in to the Income Avalanche. With fear that you won't have enough income, you make poor decisions on business prospects, accepting customers who drain energy. Doing business with inappropriate types of people doesn't work. While you are running around meeting the demands of these customers, who you have trained to take advantage of you, you could be working with people who will allow you to make an abundant living. If you haven't helped customers grow, then do so now. Make them more profitable. Maybe you could gradually raise their prices. Educate them on what makes your company more productive and hence more competitive. Train them to prosper too.

I remade my whole territory one year by asking myself: "who would you call on, who would you sell if you did not worry about money?"

TIP:

You are always harvesting something you planted, if you want a bigger harvest, Plant more!

If you'd do something different, then you could make the change. If you said, like I did, "I have the greatest job in the world, and I'd change this or that" - then write down the changes. See how you can live up to them, then give yourself a timetable to make the changes happen.

I used this plan to remake my own territory and followed with two record-setting years and the "Salesperson of the Year" award.

Starting with the end in mind, I thought about what needed improving in my territory. I wanted to deal with larger customers and make 100% more than I was making and have more time to myself to enjoy life. Next, I reviewed each customer and ranked them by sales, profit, commission and the time they required from me. I noticed that many of the low margin customers took a lot of my time. I also noticed that some of the large customers required that I showed up each week. I knew that to get more time to see new, larger customers or to increase sales in my best customers, I would have to re-arrange the time I was spending and increase the margins on many of my existing customers.

Next, I targeted those customers that had the potential to grow and those that needed a reduced call schedule and higher margins.

I set meetings with each client and told them upfront that my company wants to increase sales by 20% or more during the next 12 months. I then told them of my new plans. If it involved calling on them in person only once per month, instead of weekly, we discussed it. I asked how they felt, and together we settled on how we would make it work. I set phone calls in between, or trained some of their staff to place the orders, etc.

> **TIP:**
>
> Customers will say price determines the sale and it's not true. You determine if you get your price or not.

PRICE IS NOT WHY PEOPLE BUY.

Get your price. Here is how:

1. Start upfront with prospects by setting the expectation. I would always say, "We are not the lowest price. We focus on good service and results. Would you agree that we usually get what we pay for in life?" or "How do you price your products? Are you the lowest price provider in your business?" Usually their answer here was *no*, and I would add, "Well, neither are we". If they did answer *yes* then perhaps they would not be a fit for me and I would ask more questions to determine a fit like "Is price the only factor you use when deciding on a purchase like this?", etc.
2. Starting with the end in mind, what is the ideal margin you require to provide your customer with the level of service they expect and that aligns with your mission statement? Do the research. Where are your company's products or services priced in relation to your competition? If you are the lowest or close, why not go up 5%? Raise prices by 10% on all services and items that your customers buy because you have it or

that you sell very few of each month. They are buying because you have it or you are very good at it. What is your market share? If it's below 2% or above 30% you could raise pricing. If you are on the lower share of the market, you can raise prices because lowering 5% will not raise your market share significantly and could put you out of business. Hopefully, your service or your mission justifies the increase. If you are on the higher end of market share, determine why you have achieved that proportion of share? Perhaps you have the reputation for great service and can justify a 2 – 5% higher margin. Test it -- have your marketing staff do the survey or hire someone to do it. If they justify the increase, you can get a quick return on that investment.

Pay full price when you shop. Be willing to pay top dollar to a merchant you like. Pay for a service from a merchant who earns your trust and respect. What we give we get in life, so if you want full price, be willing to pay it. I have worked with sales people who complain about customers or prospects being focused only on price and when I inquire about how they buy something or ask them to tell me about the last time they bought a car, they often have quite a story about how they really "worked the sales person" and got a really good deal. Are you always bragging about how you got a low price?

TIP:

If price is the only reason people buy from you, look at how you buy things; practice paying full price yourself.

3. Use Intention. Albert Einstein once said, "80% of the movement of matter is intention." Intend that you will make your margin. Use affirmations to reinforce your intention. A good affirmation is "I am trusted, I give great service and I am paid full price." Get Wayne Dyers' book, *The Power of Intention*. Use your imagination. Visualize contracts signed and handshakes with those margins agreed upon. See the happy faces of your prospects. Feel what it would feel like to have outcomes like these. Use the power of your thoughts to help you create the world you envision.
4. Be prepared to say no if the price the prospect is attempting to negotiate is below your margin bottom line. Real negotiations usually begin at *no*. You could say, "That price does not work for me, (pause) it would mean we would have to cut our service somewhere. I could cut somewhere in the proposal. What would be okay to cut back on?" Walk away from it if you have to. Prospects respect your boundaries and if they do not, you do not need them. Many times I have held my line on pricing and walked, only to have the prospect either hold me from leaving or call me

up a day or so later to say, "I have a purchase order for you, would you come in to discuss the final details?"

TIP: Use your imagination, see yourself succeeding beyond your wildest dreams.

5. Read the book *Blue Ocean Strategy*. Create a Blue Ocean Strategy for your company and get your margins without hesitation because you are serving a market that has customers calling you for your expertise. You are not another "me too", selling the same product or service where price becomes the major determining factor.
6. If you decide to operate in the low price arena, get your operation lean, mean, efficient and productive; give great service, low pricing, and make a profit at the same time.

Your market, your territory is what you have made it

You can remake your company or your territory anytime you like.

Here's how:

1. Start with the end in mind, as Stephen Covey says, "Set your annual income goal."
2. What is the average sale for the territory? How many customers or sales are required to hit the goal? What if the average sale doubled? What kind of prospects or customers fit the profile of doubling the average sale? How many of the existing customers fit the profile of the increased average sale? Make a list of the existing customers that do not fit your

new profile. Determine which customers have the potential to fit your new profile over time. Perhaps they are buying from some of your competitors and you could increase your business or they are growing or have plans for expansion. Any customers that will not fit your new plan, give them to someone else in the company, perhaps a trainee or decide to make phone calls the main source of contact with your customers . You could raise their prices and just see what happens.

3. Next, using the picture of your new, ideal customer, make a list of target accounts. Ask your existing customers if they know anyone who works at these accounts and would they recommend you? Would they introduce you to them? Even if the person they know is not the decision maker, their friend or contact would probably know the decision maker or know someone at the company who does. Either way, you get to make a warm call, instead of a cold call. Next, for targets that you cannot get introduced into, develop a marketing post card, something that would get their attention concerning your product or service. Perhaps you know of a particular problem or pain that many of your customers had before you sold them. Send the post card to the target accounts (mail 20 or 25 at a time, it's easier to follow up on a small amount, remember to keep it manageable). Mail them three or four times and be sure to include the following message on the third and fourth card, "I will be calling you to ask for an appointment next week." More on warming up a call in chapter 12.

Now, make sure that you call. Your goal is to keep the mailing going with new targets so that eventually you will be calling 20 to 25targets per week, 4 or 5 per day -- manageable. Your job is action. Keep the action up and sales will increase.

TIP:

Sales behavior is planting seeds of a future harvest.

4. Cold calls. If you are going to cold call, make them outrageous. The targets should be the best of the best. Start at the top. Call the president. Who calls her or him anyway? Very few people start at the top. Call on prospects that you have previously thought would never buy from you. Even the ones that you think the competition has "sewn up". If you only make one of these calls per day, that equals five per week. Over the course of 50 weeks, that is 250 calls per year. If you only get 20 appointments and close 5, you are closing 5 of your targets from the list of the "best of the best" customers that buy what you sell. Imagine the impact of that one activity on your sales results. Imagine the impact on your income. Feel how it would feel. How would your company feel about you? Feel it. It is behavior that gets results over time. Keep working and forget about outcomes. If you are working each day and working on yourself as well, the outcomes will be positive.

CHAPTER 8: DEVELOP A SYSTEM TO FOLLOW

Prospects have been using a system designed as a defensive measure against high pressure and non-professional salespeople.

Does this sound familiar? Prospects tell you that they are very interested and ask you to tell them all about your company and what you sell. You tell them and ask for the order. They start to work you on price or ask you to do a quote or formal proposal. You do one and again ask for the order. They tell you it looks good and ask you to call back in a week or so. You do and you get stuck in what I call voice mail jail.

Prospects are either using you to get a better price from their current supplier or service provider; or they are getting free consulting.

I suggest that you use a system to help you determine if prospects are really committed to what you provide. Then you could decide to move forward or not; and you will be helping them make the same decision as well. Help them buy. You could use my suggested system that follows or develop one of your own. Remember that your prospects are using one, so be prepared.

1. BOND

Set aside 20% of the allotted time for the call to bond, unless the client shows no inclination to bond.

2. SET THE RULES OF THE CALL.

Have an outline or agenda. Tell them "to help make our time together productive, I have an agenda, would you mind if I go over it?" Tell them that you will have to ask what might seem like a lot of questions, to help them determine if you are the right company for them. Give them permission to ask you questions as well. Tell them that in your experience, most people ask a lot of questions as well and some of them are… (Suggest some questions, ones that you would like them to ask!).

3. PROVIDE PRESSURE RELIEF.

Then say, "If at any point you feel like my company is not a good fit, do you mind telling me 'no, it's not going to work'? I'm okay with *no*." After they respond, you could also add, "On the other hand, we do not do business with everyone. Would you mind if I came to the same conclusion if I said, 'Gee, I get a feeling that you are not a fit for us, do you mind if I share why?'" (This could pave the way to reopen the sale).

4. USE THE 70/30 RULE.

Use the 70/30 gauge commitment. What you are feeling, find a way to say it. Bring up your biggest fears.

Prepare questions that will encourage the prospect to talk 70% of the time. Listen and take notes to gauge for areas of pain or concern. Listen for problems that are potentially costing them lots of money if they do not fix them. Listen for problems that could cost them their job, company, or prestige if they ignore them. Listen for a desire to have a new future, unlike the past. Ask about the past, how long have they had the problem? What have they done to fix it? Has it worked? Have they told their existing supplier? What happened?
If the responses have them telling you a story of woe, ask them how they feel about that. Whatever you feel during their responses, find a way to say it and whatever your biggest fears are, bring them up.

This builds an adult-adult relationship. People will respect you for it. Refer to the communication chart in Key 9. See chart on page 35.

5. DETERMINE BUDGET.

Ask, in general terms, what have they set aside to fix the problem? If they respond with "We never share that." ask "If I said it was going to cost between X and Y, are you in that range? Closer to X?

6. DECISION, ASK ABOUT THE DECISION.

Ask "The last time you made a decision like this, what did that process look like? Will you be bringing anyone else in to help you?" (If yes, ask if they are there now, or when will they be including them in a meeting.) Suggest that typically, you attend the final decision meeting to help them all make the best decision for their business. Ask how do they see you helping them make the decision?

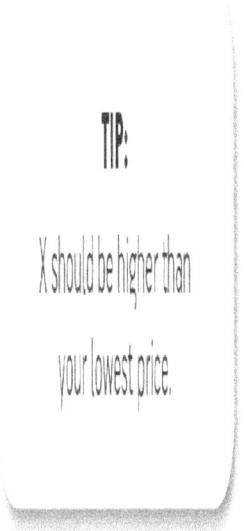

TIP:
X should be higher than your lowest price.

7. PRESENT

Present only to the needs expressed during the questioning, nothing more, and nothing less. Before you start, ask if you can go over your notes to be sure you have all of their concerns correct. Go over the list and validate their concerns, "We see this…" Ask if they have anything to add, then ask them to rank their top three of the ones you went over. You only need the top three to start your presentation. Start with the top three.

8. CLOSE.

Take the temperature first. Ask "on a scale of 0 to 10, if 0 was we would not go to the next step, and 8 was we would go to the next step, where are you on that scale?" If over 5, ask, "what would you need to hear to go to 8?" If they are below 5 ask "what would you need to hear to get to a 5? If they are at 8, simply ask, "What would you like to do next?" They will tell you how to close them.

If they are at 0, you could say, "Oh, I must have missed something, where did you feel that we were not a fit?" Listen intently as you could reopen or it could be the time to end it as well.

9. SET THE DEAL.

Be sure the deal is set. Once you close, hand the purchase order or deposit check back to the prospect before you go, and ask, "Sometimes, not very often, people change their minds for various reasons after I leave, is there anything else you think we need to cover before I take your (check or Po)?" This gives the prospect the chance to deal with buyer's remorse before you go. Did you ever leave a store thinking, "Why did I buy that?" Discover if your prospects are feeling any remorse over their decision and help them with it. If you are detached from outcomes, you can bring this up easily and prospects will thank you for it.

Remember during the whole interview, whatever you feel, whatever you fear, pay attention to it. Find a way to say it.

10. KEEP TRACK OF YOUR RESULTS.

Track how you are doing and use a system. Whether you choose this one or another, using a system can help you figure out what you may be doing wrong, but only if you track your results.

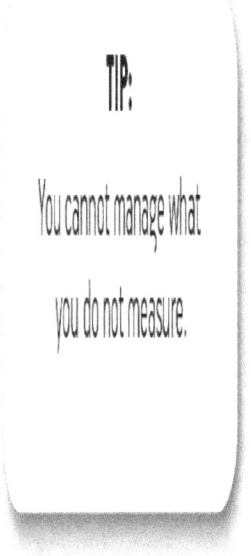

TIP:

You cannot manage what you do not measure.

CHAPTER 9: SOCIAL MEDIA – GET IT RIGHT.

I like LinkedIn and Twitter, and the rules apply for any of the social media you choose for business. What follows is my advice.

What not to do after you connect with someone.

The following is based on my experience. The events described below are real. The names have been removed to protect the innocent

1. Don't reach out to me like this after just connecting with me;

"Good evening, I just read your profile and I thought this is something you might be interested in. A reputable partner of mine is proposing to collaborate with you in a profitable business arrangement that is very much within your capacity as an individual or business owner to accomplish.

For more information, contact xxxxxxxxxxxxxxxxxxx

Awaiting your response and please all inquiry should be sent via e-mail to xxxxxxxxxx as I will be away for a family vacation. Do have a great weekend ahead.

Warm Regards. Talk about the lack of professionalism....wow...never reach out with offers to people you have not yet made a relationship with. First find out how you can help someone...remember giving first...give what you want to get.

Can you believe it? Would you accept this request? How did you feel about it while you read it? I do not know the person. Amazing, huh?

Respect your connections and get to know them first.

2. You have just connected or I have agreed to connect with you, and we do not know each other. Why would you recommend me? I am not flattered easily, and less so by people who have never met me and they

recommend me for my skills -- or management ability or sales ability. Perhaps you could recommend me for writing skills after you read some of my work, but how could you for anything else? Again, get to know me first.

3. Please don't reach out with an offer to sell me a product or service. Again, I don't know you and people buy from people they like and trust. Build trust first with an offer to help me or send me some information you think will help me. Do not sell me too early as I just dismiss all of those requests. Did you even read that I am a sales trainer and author? At least do some research and find out my philosophy of selling -- I am all over the web.

4. Download *The 7 Habits of Highly Successful Linkedin Users* by Dennis Brown or LinkedIn the Sandler Way by Sandler Sales Training at https://www.sandler.com/resources/sandler-books/linkedin-social-selling

Study how to use LinkedIn from a few experts before you do any prospecting.

I am glad to help you after you connect with me. Ask me for help; it's another way for us to get to know each other.

Then maybe we would recommend each other or refer each other.

I want to get to know you. Reach out like that and I am glad to help.

LinkedIn, Twitter or any Social Media are perfect for helping people buy. You can write articles about what you sell and how to get the best value. You can tweet articles that are related to your industry. You become visible through writing and then become credible by your content. Dr. Ivan Misner, Founder of BNI says, "Visibility + Credibility = Profitability."

As I have said, "no commission breath" -- no one cares about your need to make a quota or a raise in pay. Remember, the energy you put out comes back. What did you think about the people I wrote about above? How would you describe the energy they put out?

Relax, breathe, and add value. It will come back. You will be a respected expert in your industry over time. Malcom Gladwell wrote, "This is the scholarly tradition I was referring to in my book *Outliers*, when I wrote about the 'ten-thousand-hour rule.' No one succeeds at a high level without innate talent, I wrote: 'achievement is talent plus preparation.'" But the ten-thousand-hour research reminds us that "the closer psychologists look at the careers of the gifted, the smaller the role innate talent seems to play and the bigger the role preparation seems to play." He goes on to say, "Anyone could achieve a level of proficiency that would rival that of a professional. It was just a matter of putting in the time."

Put in the time to become an expert and people will come to you. If you push your product or your expertise, there is only one way people can go, and that is away from pushing.

When you use the great gift of productivity, along with properly using Social Media to help people buy, that energy will draw people to you.

CHAPTER 10: MULTI-LEVEL MARKETING SALES

I have been in a few multi-level marketing sales businesses. I have been solicited by many others who wanted me to participate as a "business owner" or as a customer. Many used pressure tactics "pushing me" (or thinking they were) to enroll me in their program. Telling anyone how great your program is -- how great your shake is or promising what your skin crème can do -- makes me want to puke and run away. When you sell too hard, it's now all about your goals. How do you think I feel when you are pushing to sell "your products?"

I know a few MLM folks who push, push, push. I have heard them say, "I don't get it Steve…this is a no brainer, why don't they see that and want to join in or buy the product…I just don't get it."

The only thing that these folks don't get is the history of MLM. There have been many flops along with all of the successes. Typically, MLM people approach non sales people who are uncomfortable with any kind of approaching people about anything -- it's not personal. When any kind of pressure is put on the non-sellers, they will say anything to get you away from them, including things like "Okay this sounds great, I will be doing it…call me next Tuesday and I will sign up." Or "Yes it sounds great, let me think about it and call me tomorrow."

Sound familiar?

I know they do. These kind of responses come from a lack of upfront work, softening your approach and wanting your goals more than you want to help your friend, your relative or your prospect.

If you love your MLM program, whether it's energy, shakes, vitamins or whatever, you want folks to experience what you love --and you want them to feel that. Here is how to help people experience your passion, and not your goals.

1. Make sure that this MLM is truly your passion. Make sure that you have a story, a true story, about how this work or product has changed your life. What your life was before and now after.
2. Detach from outcomes. I have talked about that in previous chapters and it is the same with MLM. You cannot control others, only yourself; so discernment and discipline is especially important now with MLM. Ask questions that bring up your biggest fears like "What have you heard about MLM's in general, how do you feel about MLM, and what experience have you had previously with people who were in a MLM and approached you? What about approaching others, how do you feel? Would you like to hear about how this has changed my life and how I feel when I help others with this? Would you like to hear about how others who I have successfully helped? How about those that did not make it?" (all MLM folks have people who have enrolled and did not do much or anything at all after enrolling). Get the point? You are curious about where your friend, relative or prospect stands and how they feel, not starting with how great your program is. It's about establishing a dialogue that helps them hear and you, if they are even a fit…help them hear their own fears and then you help them…Hopefully your program has an effective program for building a relationship not a sale. Sales will come if you follow my program or any good program. It's easy…be human, be vulnerable and be there to help.
3. Now you ask, "Would you like to hear how I help my fellow partners?" Now talk about what you do to help your fellow MLM partners succeed. Do you have such a program or are you only interested in signing folks up? Here is where the rubber meets the road -- if you are not interested in helping your downline succeed, then this is truly about your goals and your greed. Rethink this, as it will be a huge stumbling block down the

road. Create a program to help others succeed and remember, you get what you give. Success will come to you

4. "Would you like me to show you our program?" Now you show your program, all along the way asking permission to move ahead. Check by taking it away, and not as a tactic, but because you care, you ask, "How are you feeling about this so far? Would you like to say *no* now? Am I scaring you at all? Okay to move ahead?" Now you share your program in all its glory.

5. After your presentation, ask "Okay, who wants to leave?" Never be afraid of *no*. *No* helps you get those who can be a fit and a *yes* faster to *yes*. *No's* will be a *no* anyway. When would you like to know it? If anyone says "Yes, I want to leave…" you say, "Okay, would you mind sharing why and what makes you uncomfortable?" Once they answer, you could ask, "What would make you feel more comfortable? If you can reopen it, fine. Otherwise, let them go. I would ask, "Anyone else feel the same way?" When you are not afraid to have anyone in the room who does not want to be there, guess who remains? Those who are really interested and they see how that is your goal. Your true goal is to help others succeed and not to "force" anyone to sign up. Either they get it or it's okay not to.

6. Now you say to those remaining… "Okay, any other questions?" and then "Okay, those who would like to know what is next, come on up."

7. For those who do sign up, you ask, "Okay, before I complete the enrollment, are you sure, how do you feel right now? Again, you cannot lose someone who is really committed and feels the same passion and has a dream or a goal to be in the same MLM business as you. You will be amazed at how this process works, and then ask people "How was my process for you? Do you feel like you can learn it? I want you to learn how to help others decide to do this, not to sell anyone on doing this. Okay?"

If you would like me to speak to your group about this method of connecting with people, call me or email me.

Steve Lentini

Section 2
Seeds of Success

"We are always harvesting something we planted"
  — *Steve Lentini*

CHAPTER 11: USE AND UNDERSTAND THE "SEASONS"

Use the examples that Nature provides all around us for free.

Nature provides us with a powerful example of how to have an abundant harvest. In nature, we see four distinct seasons. Spring, Summer, Fall and Winter.

In Spring, the farmer prepares the ground for the planting of the seeds. The salesperson in spring is preparing the ground for his/her future success. How does a salesperson prepare the ground? Make meeting new people every day your goal, not selling them. Your purpose in spring is to prepare the ground and to plant the seeds. Resist the urge to "rush the harvest". Too often, salespeople attempt selling, or harvesting, the first time they call or meet someone. Prospects usually "pull back" from early attempts to "harvest" or sell. They feel the pressure. Would you stand over a tomato seedling and shout, "Okay now, give me a tomato!"? Of course not. We understand the cycles in nature much better than we do with people, and yet the laws are the same. Prepare the ground, plant the seed and then wait. The same goes for selling. Prepare the ground with research about where your ideal customers hang out. Then plant seeds by meeting them there, where they hang out. You can also prepare the ground with effective marketing, mailing and advertising campaigns. Good public relations and community work also helps, especially when your efforts get noticed and published in the newspapers or in the media.

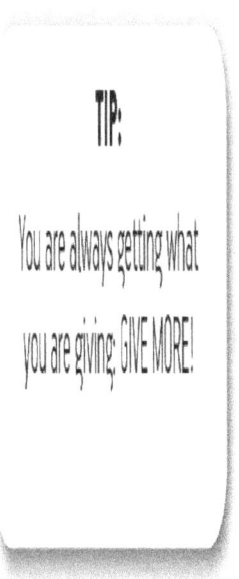

TIP:
You are always getting what you are giving; GIVE MORE!

Do the research and prepare the ground. Then plant seeds by meeting people and making relationships first. Find out how you can help people. Discipline your thoughts and judgments when you first meet people. Think only good thoughts. I silently salute the "Divinity" in each person I meet every day, and I send them my blessings as a gift or I wish them "joy, success and happiness". Thoughts have energy, so sending positive thoughts to your prospects, clients, friends and relatives couldn't hurt. Think of the times that you have called someone and noticed that they did not seem okay. How did you notice? You felt that their energy was lowered or heard something in their voice that said things weren't right. Customers and prospects will pick up on the energy that you are sending when you are thinking positive thoughts about them.

After the seeds sprout in spring, next comes the summer.

THINK CARE, NURTURE, FEED AND WEED

Summer is a time for care of the crop. The seeds of spring have broken through the hard ground. Now is the time for consistent effort. Care for your customers. Little time off and much diligence is required. Protection of the crops, nurturing, feeding, and weeding are the daily routines to provide for the growth into strong plants, or customers, that will give the bountiful harvest. Again, you will face many tests as nature deems you fit, or not, for the upcoming harvest. "Will you rail against the storms, rocks, bugs and weeds?" as Jim Rohn says in his book *The Garden of Life*. Call them unfair and unjust? If so, you are classified as one who seeks the reward without the effort, something in return for nothing. In our Cause and Effect Universe, this cannot be. If you expect something for nothing, you will reap just that. It is not unfair; it is just how it is. The Universe does not weep for your failure or celebrate your victory. If after planting your seeds, you do not see results, the lesson here is to persist through the doubt. Keep your vision. Take some time daily to visualize your goals. Imagine contracts being signed and checks coming to you. I spend time daily actually "seeing" the checks, using my imagination. I imagine the check. In my mind's eye I see "Pay to the order of." I see the amounts made out, then the written amount and the check signed. I see "handshake deals and contracts signed".

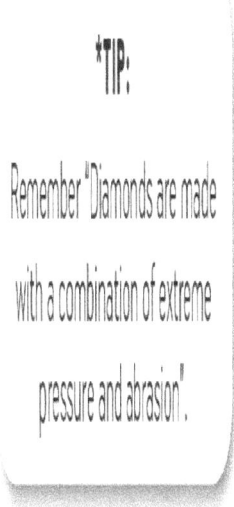

*TIP:

Remember "Diamonds are made with a combination of extreme pressure and abrasion".

Expect to be tested. You are tested, as humans grow strong by facing obstacles and difficulty. Gratitude and action is required for all of our adversity. For our character grows with adversity and in our response to it, not with inaction. As we come to expect difficulty, we can celebrate our future strength and see that in the absence of adversity, we would wither and be blown away with the first "storms of our lives".

I heard a story about the "Biosphere" in Colorado. When it first opened, under a dome, it was a grand experiment. Scientists were duplicating everything in nature under a dome to observe all the cycles of life for possible life on far away planets. The idea was that, if it worked, we could duplicate our life on barren planets, under a controlled environment like the dome. Scientists noticed the trees that were planted, would fall over when they reached between five and six feet tall. They were scrawny and not very healthy looking. They tried different foods, tested the soils, varied the temperatures and the light conditions, but nothing worked. Then, one day someone realized what had been missing. Wind! Varied winds, especially strong winds, served to break some of the roots as the trees swayed back and forth in response. Where the roots broke, new shoots formed which went deeper into the ground, serving to further anchor the tree to protect it from future high winds and storms. So to, storms and the high winds of our lives allow us to form more deeper roots. With this new appreciation for our storms, we can be grateful when they come. We can know deep down that we are being prepared and strengthened for a future bountiful harvest. What a gift.

NEXT, THE HARVEST

> **TIP:**
>
> Care for your customers. Give them the service they deserve. Feed and weed, and watch out for pests (competitors) who would take your harvest. Pay attention.

There is a long anticipated return for what we have sown. What we have now in our lives is our harvest from our previous spring. Whatever our preparation was, whatever seeds we planted, we are now reaping. If you are frustrated, unhappy, broke, unemployed or deeply in debt, you have planted the seeds of this yourself. Accept the responsibility and move on.

You could blame others for your harvest, but if you planted a garden and it withered and died, or if you neglected it and the harvest was meager, would you blame it on your employer, your parents, your spouse, your business partners, or any others? Of course not, and yet we see humans attempt to do this with their lives all the time. Until we let go of the "blame game", the victim, and the pity mode, we cannot advance to a rich and bountiful harvest. The harvest is a time to let go of things.

*TIP:

"If you don't like your experience of the world, change how the world is experiencing you."

- Steve Lentini

Just as the trees let go of the leaves, just as the blossoms and fruits fall away, we too must decide what and who to let go of in our lives. To have a new future and new harvest, we must decide to let go of old patterns and choices that have held us to this harvest of gloom. And yet this is also a reason to celebrate. Because whatever our current harvests, we can begin to plant anew.

WINTER, DON'T FORGET TO REST

Winter is our time to rest, to surrender. Surrender to the idea that things are still happening underground, although we cannot see them. Before planting anew, after any harvest, a time of reflection is required. Winter is a time of learning too. A time for seminars, classes and study of what could be next. Meditation about what did not work in the last harvest, what did, and preparation and planning for the next planting is important too. Winter is a good time for journaling. Write down what the recent harvest brought in to the storehouse or the lack of it. Tie the resultant harvest back to the activities and action we took in spring. Notice any patterns of self-doubt and defeat. Look for the "blame game" and victim dialogue within yourself. Even if you have just had a bountiful harvest, one cannot assume that this pattern will repeat. You must take the same care with planting the next crop, selecting the site, soil, and seeds carefully, so as to ensure another bountiful harvest.

We humans are built to grow, expand and produce. We are happiest when we are risking and reaching deep down within ourselves, using all of our gifts. Magnanimity is joyful. Pusillanimity is not. Pusillanimity is holding back one's gifts. The Universe knows that you are holding out. Dare and dream big. Believe. Now is the time to prepare for when the earth warms and the soil loosens. Getting ready for the slip and slide from the mud of spring, the high winds and the rains.

Preparation now will make winters enjoyable as you will see the need for winter in your cycle. You will understand winter's role and be grateful for it. Unlike our western society, where rest is scorned, you will come to value it as you rest and prepare for the next planting, while others are still running around wondering what just happened in the last harvest -- not even aware that the cycles and seasons of nature are here to teach, instruct and even comfort us. We can be comforted knowing that cycles and seasons are normal and a part of our lives as well,not just something to go through or complain about each year.*

*information on the seasons comes from Toni Stone, c/o Wonder Works Studio, 401 Buck Hollow Road, Fairfax, Vt, wwwwonderworks.org and from Jim Rohn's book *The Seasons of Life*

CHAPTER 12: SET TIME AND BOUNDARIES AND SELL ONLY THE BEST OF THE BEST.

Set your goals high enough and be strong enough to eliminate time-wasting customers and prospects from your list. Train customers to respect your time. Your time is too valuable to waste on people who lack the respect you need. You need the time to respond to your good customers and good targets. Thinking like a lawyer or an accountant can help -- both track their time and charge by the minute. When you are in front of a customer or answering an urgent call from a client, set the clock and measure the financial return you are getting for the time invested. The customer at the bottom of your list needs a boost or perhaps you can start a junior salesperson on his or her way in your company. This does not mean that you "rush" prospects or customers. You cannot manage what you do not measure. So be aware of people who are time wasters. You can assign inside sales to help with smaller customers, offer them to your boss and ask for his or her advice, (the boss will love that you are focusing on being more productive).

Setting priorities help you establish boundaries around what you are willing to spend time on and with whom. Once you have established boundaries, you can say no to the prospects, customers, and situations that do not fit with the established priorities. Many sales and business people who are mired in a rut or not as successful as they wish, often cannot say no or are people pleasers. People pleasers lack the self-respect to set boundaries. I speak with business owners whose main lament is that they have experienced salespeople that have hit a plateau and have been stuck at or near the same sales levels for many years. When confronted with their mediocrity, they defend themselves with excuses like, "Well, if there weren't so many backorders," or "The competition is killing us." "The installers are always late" or "The programmers never deliver the new upgrade on time." Whatever the excuse, that is just what it is, an excuse. They cannot see that they are the block and the main reason for the sales plateau.

If you are one of the above, step back and look at all the excuses that have held you back. Stop wasting time pleasing customers. Stop doing busy work to excuse yourself from making new calls, joining an association of your peers, networking or pursuing any other productive work.

TIP:

Read The Power of a Positive No by William Ury.

Setting boundaries and saying *no* will be uncomfortable at first. Practice with low risk scenarios and people. Notice how you feel the first time you say *no*. Your self-respect will increase. Then as you increase your free time, be sure to invest it wisely. Time is a salesperson's inventory. Manage it wisely by setting priorities and boundaries.

We NEVER have to settle for less than the best of the best.

HOW DO WE GET THE BEST OF THE BEST, YOU ASK?

1. Start with the end in mind. What is the ideal prospect or customer for your business? Who is the ideal? What makes your company the best of the best to serve their market? Do whatever it takes, spend whatever time or money, and set your company up to serve the best of the best if you are not suited to serve that market now. Why would the best of the best buy from you? Understanding who your ideal customer is and how you are the best at serving them helps you prepare questions that will determine if they are a fit for you and you for them. You are doing both parties a favor by uncovering what is the ideal supplier or company to serve their needs. How can you walk away if you are uncertain of what will absolutely NOT work for you?

2. Be certain about when to walk away. Certainty is not only necessary, it is absolute here. You cannot waiver on this. You could decide to set up a trial if you are feeling like a prospect could be a fit -- a trial with the upfront understanding that you are trying them out, that you are uncertain if you are the best fit for them. Explain upfront in the call, that

you are going to ask a lot of questions because you are there to help them find the best fit, NOT TO SELL THEM ANYTHING. Tell them you are there to help them buy the best solution, even if it is not you. You could also tell them that you do not sell everyone and ask, "Is it ok with you if, at some point, I feel that we are not a fit for each other, that I tell you?"

TIP:
Your goal is to look different from your competition.

Buyers today are very sophisticated. Chances are they have already done a lot of research about their choices in the market before they invited you in. The old days of selling are over. People buy from people they like and trust, and you build trust by being open and honest. People are relieved when you help them buy; if they do not buy from you today, they will tomorrow or they will refer you. I have often consulted software companies and their customers' biggest complaints are that they lie about everything -- delivery dates, the cost of writing extras to the program, service times, everything. Imagine their reaction to a salesperson that told them upfront things like "We are not the best at delivery times. Sometimes we take over six months to deliver special fixes to the software. How do you feel about that?" Most of the competitors are lying saying things like "Oh, we get the extras written in no time... just a few days." My clients tell the truth and their sales explode. Who doesn't want to buy from someone who is honest?

3. Detach from the outcome. You will not say *no* to a prospect if you are tied to your goals or the bills that are due. Let it go and you will attract what you want. You won't until you do, so do it now. When you let it go and say *no* to people who are not a fit, the Universe responds to your certainty. You will get the reputation of serving only the best of the best. I only help those who are truly dedicated to taking their "self" on -- those totally dedicated to being the best of the best -- and today, people pay me $2,500, $5,000, $20,000 and more to help them improve. I have clients committing to my programs for two, three and four years or more. Do you think this would be happening if I had continued to say *yes* to everyone?

TIP: Be different by being open and honest.

4. Set your price and stick to it. That will help you say *no*. If they say, "You're too high," you can say, "Well, that is my price, what do we do now?" Before you go, you can ask, "What is your experience in the past when you have gone with the cheapest solution?" All you want to do here is to have them hear, in their own words, whether the lower cost provider has been the best choice in the past. It could begin a new dialogue about what your "best of the best" services would bring them. If not, you cannot lose what you did not have. Walk away certain, sure and assured, knowing that the "best of the best" are on their way to you.

5. Spend some time each day, at the beginning or end, or both if you can, visualizing and meditating on how the best of the best customer would look and feel. Practice visioning -- spending some time quietly receiving a vision on how the future will be or on what direction or decision to make. See in your imagination, large contracts, happy customers, and big checks with your name on them. See you being stretched and challenged by these "best of the best" clients. Feel how it would feel to win these great clients. Feel how it would feel if you only targeted and won the best of the best. How much of the market share do you have? 1%, 2%, not even 1/10 of 1%? If that's the case, why are you targeting the lowest 1/10th? Why aren't you starting at the top of your market? IF YOU ARE ONLY GOING TO SERVE 1% OF YOUR MARKET TOPS, WHY ARE YOU OPERATING AT THE BOTTOM?

Try this out for two years.

Start with the end in mind; define what the best of the best looks like. Set your company up to serve the best of the best if you are not yet capable. Be certain of your new direction. Who do you prefer to buy from -- confident, assured and certain people or wishy-washy dish rags that work for anyone? Or for any amount? Set your price. Detach from outcomes and be prepared to walk away. *No*, will never sound better, when it comes from you or them, if you will not budge and are certain. Spend quiet time seeing your goal, feeling how it will feel when it happens.

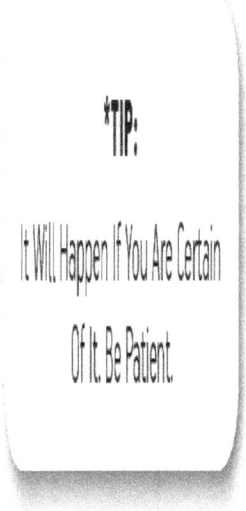

*TIP:

It Will Happen If You Are Certain Of It. Be Patient.

Remember, if you only have 1/10 of 1% of the market, which end makes the most sense to spend your resources on?

Who deserves it more?

I can't think of anyone better, can you?

CHAPTER 13: DEAL CHEERFULLY WITH OBJECTIONS AND COMPLAINTS.

I believe that sales people should not deal with an objection until the prospect has had an opportunity to deal with it first. Typical sales people answer every question they are asked. If you say something that might kill the sale, the prospect will usually not share that information until you are chasing them through voice mail. Let's look at two scenarios.

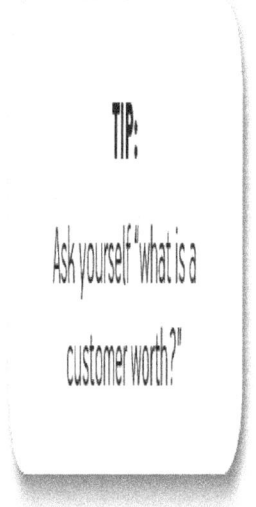

Scenario 1.

Prospect: Is your machine guaranteed?

Typical Sales person: Yes, it has a one-year guarantee.

Prospect: One year? I just looked at a competitor's machine and their guarantee is two years.

Scenario 2.

Prospect: Is your machine guaranteed?

You: Yes, what type of guarantee are you looking for?

This is called a reverse. Reversing a question before you answer, or after you have given a very short answer, helps you determine why the prospect asked that. Why did they bring that up just then?

Scenario one leaves you in a box. Scenario two leaves the door open for you to try to match the prospect's expectations. Try using scenario two from now on and see if it makes selling a little easier. Whatever you are asked, ask them about it. If you slow down and listen, you will remember to ask about the question rather than answer it and possibly lose their trust, make them uncomfortable and lose the sale. Reversing the question usually works very well. If someone asked you about your terms, you could say, "What kind of terms are you looking for?" "How long does it take for support staff to learn your new program?" You would reverse by saying "What time frame would work best to teach your support staff?"

Whatever you are asked, you reverse the question to help you structure an offer that fits what the prospect wants, or it will help you understand if their expectations are unreasonable. The negotiation can begin then or you could choose to end the process. Either way, you are always working on the truth.

> **TIP:** You reverse a question because it's not important what you think on a sales call or what you think the solution is; it's most important to find out what the prospect thinks.

In this Universe that we live in, physicists are now saying that creation happens in the space between things. If you are listening, without having to jump in with your remarks or defending, things can happen in the space you create by listening. By listening and leaving some silence before you speak, you are allowing the space for your customer or prospect to feel heard. When we feel heard or listened to, we feel better. Whether you are resolving a dispute or listening to a prospect object to some part of your offering, listen and leave some silence in between your responses and allow something new to be created. Sometimes prospects will solve the objection themselves or an upset client will suggest the solution to a problem that will satisfy them.

TIP: Silence creates the space for miracles to occur.

Step back, listen and wait. Watch what happens. Every day, I work on listening and leaving space for others to have their position. Great things have happened when all I did was listen.

When your customers call you, make sure you respond quickly. Remember, procrastination has a cost. I have a client who is always procrastinating with his customers. He makes promises and is always late or forgets completely to deliver what he has promised. He usually ends up with gigantic problems that cost him a lot of money to fix. He has to give big discounts to keep people from being really mad at him or worse, he loses the customer. Service is 80% of sales. Not only does this show the customers that you value their time, it also demonstrates respect and professionalism.

TIP:

Respond to complaints cheerfully and resolve quickly; response equals respect.

Remember, you do not have to fix everything in that moment -- don't promise too much. Give yourself time -- under promise - over deliver. The customer will appreciate your quick response. By delaying your response, you usually end up with infuriated customers.

Give your customers your car phone, home phone, beeper, etc. In my 30 years of sales, few ever called me at home.

Resolve problems quickly. Remember the following:

»Expect problems

»Quickly respond to an angry customer

»Remember, under promise - over deliver

When you get on the road every day, expect problems. By expecting problems, you are not surprised or upset once they occur. When you are upset, you are wasting the time and energy that could be spent solving the problem. If similar problems continuously occur, bring them to the attention of management. If you are the individual running the show, get your operational staff on the job.

But again, do expect problems on a daily basis, even anticipate what they will be. This way, you will be mentally prepared to stay upbeat. You will not be defeated by any problems because you will be prepared. When a customer has a complaint, respond quickly. A quick response defuses an angry customer. By delaying your response, it usually upsets the customer even more. Remember, "Nothing worthwhile in life is gained by avoiding what is uncomfortable initially".** Hit problems head on; it's never as bad as you think. Always remember to under promise and over deliver. Give yourself as much time as you can get to fix the problem - if the customer needs something right away, attend to it. Do whatever it takes. If you delay, you are making things worse.

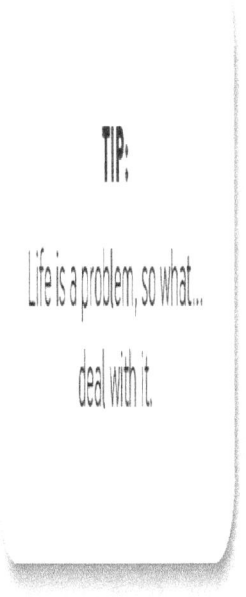

TIP:
Life is a problem, so what... deal with it.

If you do get a call or if you call on a customer who is upset with you or your company, use the following do's and don't's for successful dispute resolution.

** Steve Lentini

DO'S

»Listen intently and take notes

- »Before you respond, take a moment or two to allow silence, create space, and then say something like "I'm sorry to hear that"
- »Use *we* a lot, "We apologize, we goofed", etc.
- »"Uh oh! We did what?"
- »"I'm not sure I would buy from us."
- »Anything else?
- »"What can I do to fix it for you?" Or "What would you like us to do to fix it?"
- »Follow up with a written memo to the customer with steps taken and cc to departments involved.
- »Under Promise and over deliver here.
- »Get back to the customer again within a week to follow up.

DON'TS

- »Talk too much
- »Talk over the customer
- »No defending. Defending says you are right and they are wrong. Never make anyone wrong, they are the customer.
- »"I'm sorry, it will never happen again" (how can you be sure and what if it did?)
- »"We've already fixed it."
- »"That darn warehouse or driver"
- »Never use the word "they"

> **TIP:** Ask yourself "What does a customer cost?" when considering the solution to a problem or issue.

Research shows that the cost of acquiring a customer today has gone up for all industries. Depending on your industry, it could be anywhere from $500 to $50,000 or more. Teach your staff and remember this when an issue arises. Wouldn't it make sense to resolve a $500 issue quickly for a customer that costs $10,000 to acquire?

DO THE MATH.

Remember to "fall back" during an exchange with an angry or upset customer. Take the hit early on. Suggest if it fits, that you might have made the mistake. Do not propose solutions; let the customer suggest how they would like it fixed. Follow up and you will keep that customer.

Just like in dealing with objections, create space here for something to happen by allowing silence. Those uncomfortable moments when no one speaks are perfect for dispute resolution as well. Silence tells the prospect that you are taking in everything that they are saying. Many times they will offer the solution to someone who is listening and reasonable.

Bring up your biggest fears. With customers who are very upset at a repeating mistake or numerous different mistakes, I would fear losing their business. So I started bringing up that fear. I would say, after allowing them to blow off steam, "Ken, you are very upset and I agree and understand, you should be. I am a little uncomfortable right now….. (pause), I am sensing that you are so upset that this is going to get in the way of us doing business going forward."

Every time that I brought up my biggest fear, I got to answer their biggest concerns. Sometimes customers would say right then, "No, I know you are going to fix this and we are going to do business", or they would say, " No, I'm not saying that, we are still going to do business." Or sometimes they would say "Well, I might go elsewhere. Here are my concerns…"At that point, I listened intently and wrote down what they said. That was the solution to continuing to do business. I never lost a customer when I brought up my biggest fear, in fact, it was only when I didn't that we lost the business; because we left something unsaid and unresolved. By bringing up my biggest fear, we were discussing what we were both thinking anyway. We were able to discuss the solution as a result -- their solution.

When a customer gave their concerns, I would respond by saying, "What if we could only do 50% of what you are asking? What if 70%? What if 90%?" I never promised 100%, because after all, we had just made multiple mistakes, would you believe someone who made those kinds of promises? By bringing up my fear that we might only fix 50% or 70% or 90%, I knew and they heard themselves say what they would do. We both knew when I left, what I had to do to ensure that I kept the business. I made sure we did it, we delivered, and we kept the business. I also had under promised and left room for us to over deliver.

CHAPTER 14: WHEN NETWORKING AND PROSPECTING, USE YOUR CONTACTS

I once worked for a company that needed quick sales growth and the President's father had a contact in a large potential customer that we wanted badly. I'll never forget that call in my life.

On the day of the appointment, we spent three minutes or less on small talk, even though Arthur could have spent an hour catching up with his old friend. I almost fell off of my chair when Arthur asked, "Would you give my friend, Steve, some business?" - Now his friend had two options, either *yes* or *no*. He said, "yes"!

It might have taken me six months to get to that point with this very large company, but Arthur knew he could be direct with his very good business friend. I use this story often when I'm in front of a group of salespeople because it illustrates the value of using contacts and referrals. Going over your contact list every three to six months and asking your customers, friends, and acquaintances for referrals should be on going. Use any "tool" in your toolbox to shorten that decision cycle. Offer your help on a regular basis to your contacts. Watch out for business opportunities for your clients. Give them referrals often. You get what you give.

Help others with your contacts, Ralph Waldo Emerson, in his "Essay on Compensation" said, "The undisputable law of this Universe is that you get what you give."(There's that law again). If you want people to give you referrals, give them. Your book antennae should always be up for opportunities to help others. Help your customers and prospects that you meet do more business; be ready to introduce others to them that will help them. Help other sales people that you know grow their business and they will want to help you.

Networking fits in with this strategy because it's giving to others. In networking, you shall reap as you sow. Cold calling is a waste of time, in my opinion. The return for the time spent is often very low when you add in the burn out factor. Sales people, who rely solely on cold calling, burn out and turnover at a very high rate. We know this and yet most sales training is still focused on cold calling. If you are going to cold call, make it five a day on outrageously big targets. Set your sights on the biggest and best customers you can dream of and cold call them. Call the President. That way, the risk and reward ratio makes the effort worthwhile.

The same could apply to your networking. You could be working with the best and brightest in similar industries, helping them to get business. Sowing this, you would reap, over time, a harvest of the best and brightest people helping you and introducing you to new prospects. The difference is that with networking, you would be invited in, and perhaps even personally introduced, at a lunch or dinner meeting. Even one warm call a week would beat the best week of cold calling. The key to effective networking is effective sowing. I hear people complain "I'm not getting anything from my group." What do you think they sowed in spring to reap a harvest of "not getting anything"? The rule does not apply sometimes; it applies every time. As Dr. Ivan Misner, founder of BNI (Business Networking International) says, "Givers Gain. That is the motto of BNI."

Start by selecting your sites to plant. Would you plant a garden in a field of rocks, thorns, trees and scrub bushes? Do some research; ask questions. Look for groups that fit your particular occupation or business. Once selected, attend a few meetings to be sure that they call on similar types of customers and do not compete with you. How do they present themselves? How do they dress? Do they behave professionally? Would you refer these people? What are they sowing in the world? If they are sloppy and careless with their dress and their words, what kind of clients and prospects do you think are part of their harvest? Take your time here and do the due diligence. When you have found the group that fits, plant the seed and join. Now begins the springtime of your membership. Things will look messy here. The beginning of your membership in any group will feel that way. Take time here to plant deeply and carefully. Meet each member out for breakfast or lunch. Find out how you can help them. Be prepared for the meeting. Show them how professional you are. Keep your word and do everything you say you will do, even if it hurts. Do not break appointments, arrive late, or worse, arrive unprepared. Take notes in your meeting. Note the personal facts like birthdays, anniversaries, children's names, spouse name, and quirky facts that you can acknowledge at a later date. Remember, you are sowing here. Also, be aware during the meeting if the person is interested in what you do. Are they asking how they could help you? Remember, they will be showing you how they sow a crop as well. If they do not reflect the kind of crop that you want to plant, offer to help them with some ideas that you have about growing their business or better, give them this book. If they still do not fit, tell them why, and if they are open to help, give it. If not, move on to preserve your future harvest. If you feel good about working with the person, work on getting them a referral or introduction. Offer to link their website to yours. Feature them or their business in your newsletter. Send a personal letter introducing them to your top 10 customers. As you work to help them plant, so will you reap the same. Be patient. No rushing to the harvest.

Instead of joining a group to network in, you could do the same with a few respected business people who you know or would like to know, that call on the same types of customers as you and you do not compete with them. You could call them and say that you respect them, have heard great things about them, and that you call on similar types of customers. Note that you do not compete and that you were thinking that you could help them grow their business. Suggest that you meet for lunch. Start the same process as above. The goal would be to find four or five people that you could work with to develop what BNI calls a contact sphere.

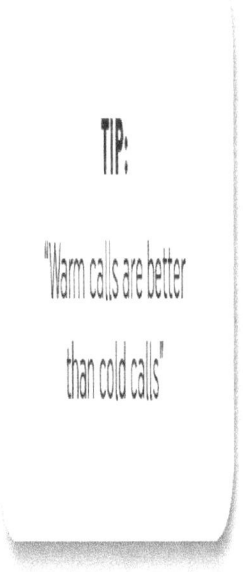

TIP:
"Warm calls are better than cold calls"

The key to prospecting is setting a goal of "warming up" the calls. Offer seminars that educate your prospect; do not sell at these events. Warm calls require that you get to know your prospect, and they get to know you. Whatever your industry, offer an informative seminar educating on an important aspect of what you do. Give real information. What you give, you get. When you give real information, your prospects will learn something and appreciate that you did not attempt to sell them. At the beginning of the seminar, ask the attendees to take out a business card and turn it over. Ask them to put the letters Y N TIO on the card. At the end of the seminar tell them what the letters stand for. Y = yes, N = no, TIO = think it over. Tell them to cross out think it over unless they are willing to accept a call from you within 48 hours and tell you *yes* or *no*. Under those circumstances, it would be okay to circle TIO. If not, then they must circle *Yes* or *No*. Tell the *no*'s you will call to ask what they liked about the seminar and to ask what could have been improved. Tell them that they can circle *yes* if they would like to hear more about what you taught them. Tell them that you will call to set an appointment.

Design a post card that you can mail to target prospects. Most people at least look at a postcard to decide whether to throw it out or not. Mail it to the top 15 or 20 prospects on your list each week for four weeks and then call. You can ask if they have gotten your post card. You can ask if they remember throwing out the one that looked like yours. Again the goal is to warm up the call.

Go over your customer list and ask for referrals. Do this every six months or so. Ask your top customers how you can help them get business. What is it that they are looking for? You cannot do this for everyone, although your top customers would appreciate a referral too. And remember, you get what you give.

Think of ways to warm up the call first, then call.

TIP:

Make your daily goal to meet new people and HAVE FUN.

By making your daily goal of meeting say five new people that you can discover whether or not they ever buy what you sell, you take the pressure off of yourself to sell something right away. You are new at selling, so the more people you meet and ask, "How can I help you?", you begin building a network of new contacts that will get to know you. You can think of it as "I am having fun meeting people that I can help and will help me someday". You can ask the new people you meet, things like "What do you look for in an ideal customer?" Ask them about their business, how have they been doing it, how did they get started, how did they get their current position, etc. Get to know them. Remember, you're developing a relationship, not making a sale – at least not yet.

What better way to operate then to make it your goal to meet new people? You do not suffer any rejection.

Ask them for help. You could say, "I am just starting out and I am looking for advice on how to grow my business, who would you call on if you were me?"

Most important of all, have FUN! Look forward to who you will meet each day and with wonder about who you might meet. Keep a smile on your face and let the world know you are having fun. See what that kind of enthusiasm will bring you.

Cold call five top prospects each day. Since cold calling has the lowest odds of success, make your targets *outrageous*. Cold call accounts that you only dream about. Remember, your dreams can come true. Why not start here?

TIP:

"When you cold call, make them BIG, real BIG."

Call at the top (who calls the president anyway?). Cold call only the top prospects in your targeted market. Since the odds aren't great, go for it. With 25 calls per week on top prospects, even with a 2% return on 1,250 calls annually, that would give you 25 appointments with the top prospects in your market.

Russell Conwell used to say, "There are diamonds in your backyard." Your diamond mine is your customer list. Mine it weekly or monthly depending on how large the list is. Ask your customers "Who do you know who might introduce me to a company I want to do business with or who could you recommend me to?" These diamonds are sitting on the ground, compared to cold calling. With cold calling, you have to dig the mine first. Referrals from your existing customers are like diamonds in a stream. If you have dealt with everyone with integrity and given to each what you want to get, if you have left everyone a little better than you found them in every moment, your customers will gladly help. You will get what you have been giving.

CHAPTER 15: DEVELOP NEW BEHAVIORS/ LOVE BEING BETTER THAN YOU WERE YESTERDAY

Don't wait for management to review you – Ask yourself, what did I do today to:

»Get closer to my goals?

»Get closer to my income needs?

»Train my customers?

»Get more productivity and customers?

Great sales people review themselves constantly! I used to wonder why salespeople who worked for me, waited for me to review them, and quite frankly, I wondered why I needed them.

One of the reasons that someone might want to review themselves daily would be the goal of "Personal Improvement". We all have personal habits that are holding our sales back. Jim Rohn, the powerful motivational speaker and the nation's premier business philosopher, has said the harder he works on himself, the better his business does. Ask your boss for the things he or she would like to see you improve; ask your family and friends as well. Most of the things you will hear, you already knew deep down inside, but until you take inventory, you won't improve. Next, prioritize that list starting with number one. Ask your prospects what went wrong after a lost sale, or what they liked about your competitor's offering.

Once you've set your sights on your personal improvement, be patient with yourself. Work on one at a time. Visualize yourself doing the new behavior you're looking for.

I can't count the number of times I've heard a salesperson or even sales managers categorize their employees as one type of sales person or another. Does this sound familiar? He or she is not a

»Detail orientated person

»Organized person

»Closer

»Opener

»Maintainer

Aren't these the actual things that are holding you back? Be honest. Never accept these things as the "Proverbial You." Remember, you become what you think about. Change them. You can. Think instead "What do I want to become?" and starting with the end in mind, think about what new behaviors would be required to become that type of person and begin to act like you are that person now. Those new behaviors would become your new habits in as soon as 21 days. Do it.

Say this to yourself daily. Tell your boss that you love being better. Make it your focus and the little things will become easier, instead of being tremendous annoyances.

People love doing business with people who are good at what they do. So, make it your goal to be better every day. Your customers, boss, and co-workers will notice and respect you.

TIP:
You are what you say you are.

All those around you will want to do what they can to help you. They will want to do it well because they know that you do things well.

If you are sloppy, don't be surprised if your support team is sloppy. If customers recognize that you are haphazard, don't be surprised if they take advantage of this.

But if you work at being the best every day (try it), you'll be amazed at how this affects, in a wonderful positive way, those around you. Try it at home as well. Your family will react positively towards you as well. By loving being better, you'll find each day will be more fun.

TIP:

"Love Being Better"

Work with passion. All too often we choose jobs that we do not love - that do not fill us with passion. We take our lunch pail and work like "serfs in the kingdom" for our masters.

Love what you do -- jobs without passion dry the blood in our veins, make our bones brittle and worse, break our souls. If selling is what you can do with a passion, then do it. If not, find the passion. Eleanor Roosevelt once said, "You must do the one thing that you think you cannot do!" Think about how that might change your life. Just Do It.

My goal each day is to leave everyone and everything a little better than I find them. This helps me be fully present in each moment. I do not have to worry about the future or regret the past if I am fully focused on the present. This is the only moment that we ever have. If I am fully present in every moment, the future takes care of itself. I have my goals and dreams and I am only focused on the moment that I have before me.

When you are always doing your best, you are in "use", honoring your Source, God, the Divine or whatever your Higher Power is for you. You are building your Universal resume. Giving your best means you will get the best in return.

A busy body in sales should be just that, busy with their business and not that of others. I call it the "general manager of the universe syndrome." Mind your own business. Stay out of the office gossip and politics. I once worked with a group of people who spent more time doing other people's jobs and engaging in office politics. This was a terrible waste of energy and their sales showed it.

Of course, by talking about everyone else, they were deflecting blame from themselves, but the truth was that the result each of these people was getting was lackluster. Let me share with you a quote from Gandhi:

"A true soldier does not argue as he marches, how success is going to be ultimately achieved. But he is confident that if only he plays his humble part well, somehow or other the battle will be won. It is in that spirit that every one of us to know how to do our own part well!"

TIP:
"Manage your life, not the lives of others"

Make written comments and suggestions every quarter to your management. This is a professional's method of contributing. Stay out of office politics.

Imagine the energy it takes to manage all the affairs of those around you. Some people are "drama addicts." They spend a considerable amount of their time caught up in other people's drama. Jeffrey Gittomer, in his book *The Little Red Book of Selling* says, "The less time you spend in other people's business and other people's drama, the more time you'll have for your own success."

I realized, about 10 years ago or so, that I could have so much more time in my life if I spent more time managing my life and less time managing the lives of those around me. People and events were things that I could not control anyway, so why waste the time and energy? I decided to give it up.

From that moment on, I spent most of my energy managing me. Now, mind you, I say most of my energy. I am human and I do catch myself in the drama of others from time to time. I notice it faster and as soon as I do, I get back on track. Many people around me note that I accomplish much and have a lot on my plate. It's not difficult for me to manage more because I am only managing my stuff most of the time. Those same people complain that they do not have enough time. If they gave up their role as "general manager of the universe" they would add enormous amounts of time and energy to their day. What they accomplish in life would increase dramatically. The minute you go in a new direction and make a new choice, new results appear. It's a law of the Universe -- the Universal Law of Cause and Effect. More on that law later.

CHAPTER 16: REMEMBER THAT "WHAT GOES AROUND, COMES AROUND"

Look in the mirror, wherever you are in your sales career, you are responsible for it. You are just where you should be according to your thoughts and actions. Accept it. Don't beat yourself up over it, but face it. Others are not to blame; the company is not to blame, nor your co-workers, and not your parents - YOU ARE. Remember this: "Incompetents invariably make trouble for people other than themselves!" © by Larry McMurtry

TIP:

You are the creator of your life.

Whenever I work with people who are blaming everyone in their company for their lack of performance, I like to hand them a mirror. People who are always blaming others for their lack of success are only deflecting the blame from themselves. So, accept it -- it's yours -- then move on. You are the creator of your life. Warner Erhard once said, "I accuse you of being a circumstance in your life". If you are a circumstance, then you are in "victim" mode. If you believe that things are happening to you, then you are in victim mode. Things have not happened to you, you have created these events. You are attracting the events and people that you need to see, in order to grow. That's why it happens that certain events or people continually show up in our lives.

Until we see it and learn a new behavior, we are destined to repeat the events or meet similar types of people. You cannot grow until you accept the responsibility, but don't linger over it. Instead, learn from your past in fact, laugh. Yes, laugh at your past, (you're not the only one with a past) then write down some goals for personal improvement. Do you think that professional athletes linger long over the missed putt, the crash on the first turn, the strike out, the fumble, the wild pitch? The successful ones certainly do not. Just keep your eyes on where you intend to be, not on where you have been. Use the past as a lesson or sign posts, so that you do not take that same road over and over. Here is a poem that I wrote over ten years ago for people who worked for me (at least that is what I thought, back when I wrote it). I came to realize a few years later that I wrote it for me. I was the biggest obstacle in my life and I had my head in a bad place as you will see.

IT CAN'T BE ME

By Stephen P. Lentini

Lots of people do better than me

I bitch and moan, kick and scream, I am unable to reach my dream.

I work hard, I think I'm smart

It's those around me, it's their part.

They're the reason, I've failed to start.

They keep me down I know it's true

At every turn, it's me they screw.

And so it goes, every day, I get Up and I'm on my way.

Convinced I'm not to blame - it can't be me, what a shame!

Wait, was that a mirror I just passed, no way, can't be, that person had their head up their a_ _!

"Respect nature and learn from the seasons"

> **TIP:**
> "Remember, you reap what you sow. What goes around comes around"

What is the result now of your last springtime? Are you reaping a bountiful harvest? What are you currently harvesting in the direct result of the quality and amount of "seeding" that you did last spring? Did you select the proper soil? Did you neglect to inspect the seeds? Did you take proper care to prepare the ground before planting? Nature provides us with a perfect model to follow and yet we humans think that these same patterns do not apply to our lives. We expect to reap a bountiful harvest even though we rested or procrastinated when we should have been planting. Think about the kind of harvest you want before you plant. Sow lies, reap lies. Sow lack of integrity, reap a lack of integrity in return. Sow procrastination, reap a bleak future. Sow honesty, reap honesty. Sow loyalty and commitment, reap loyalty and commitment in return. The one thing that we forget is that nature returns more than what is sowed by many thousand times over. Just think, from that one tomato seed you sow, the tomato plant returns thousands of seeds. The same is true in our lives. The Law is the Law. Jim Rohn says in his book *The Seasons of Life*, "Faith further provides to us an irrevocable law decreed in heaven which assures that for every disciplined human effort we will receive a multiple reward…for each cup planted, a bushel reaped." Whatever we choose to put into the soil of life will surely return to us multiplied. That is why, if we sow inaction, we reap a future of despair. What are you sowing in your business or on the job? What about at home and with your family and friends? Can you honestly say that you sow love, forgiveness, gratitude and understanding? What would the harvest be from seeds such as these, especially with the guarantee of a multiplied return?

What you expect to harvest begins with the seeds and the discipline of preparing and planting in the spring. It's never too late to begin planting anew. Start now. After planting your seeds of your new future, resist the urge to "rush to the harvest". Humans always want to rush to harvest in their lives. Would you plant an apple tree seed and then stand over it saying "Okay, where are the apples?" No, of course we wouldn't. It sounds ridiculous, and yet that is exactly what we do in our lives. Very often, we expect quick results or riches. We want to "rush to the harvest". Instead, during your winter of planning for your next harvest, write down, in addition to what seeds you will plant, a plan for nurturing the crop. Allow enough time for your seeds to sprout, grow and develop a young crop, and then a bountiful harvest is more likely. Allow time for the full cycle of seasons, one cannot rush nature and that is her message for us as well. Also, allow for bugs and pests, (negative events and people), an early frost, or any bad weather. In this way, you will not be deterred from your plan of a bountiful harvest. Spring is a time for persistence and perseverance. In my sales training and seminars over the last 7 years, I have often asked my clients, "What would spring look like if the daffodils, crocus and tulips said 'oh, there's too many rocks in the way, the ground is too hard, or it's too cold, I think I'll quit'." Do not quit when it looks like things are difficult.

> **TIP:**
>
> The Universe tests everything purposefully, to eliminate those that would give in and to weed out the ones that do not belong. You will be tested. The tests firm our resolve, if we do not give in.

There are tools required to prepare the ground and to plant properly. Just as the farmer requires the proper tools and equipment to prepare and plant, so to it is with us. The tools required for a good planting are a positive attitude, giving what we want to get, action, forgiveness, patience, love, gratitude, opening up, measuring and tracking, visualization, acting as if, speaking as if, change and awareness of choice. All of these things together will bring us a new harvest -- one unlike the past. Without choice and change, we would use all of the other tools to sow, but we would reap the same past harvest over and over. We must be willing to expand and go beyond where we have sown before, with all of the above, for each of the tools mentioned are separate crops as well. Depending on how you use them, you are sowing a future harvest from each of them. Whatever we sow in forgiveness for example, we reap when we require forgiveness ourselves. Whatever we have sown in love, patience or action, we too have reaped. If we work continually to expand where we have gone before, like the Universe is expanding, we will reap a harvest of many new benefits. Jim Rohn says in his book *The Seasons of Life*,

"The act of planting during the warm breezes of spring requires that we exert the pain of human discipline and being unwilling to do so assures that in the coming fall, we shall surely experience the greater pain of regret – the difference is that the pain of discipline weighs ounces, and the pain of regret weighs tons. We must either plant during the springtime of our life, or beg from others during the fall."

Prosperity is related to what you are thinking about in every moment.

TIP:

"GIVE what you want to get" (are you getting the message?)

Your outer world reflects your inner world. Remember what Earl Nightingale said, "You become what you think about." If your predominant thought pattern is about being frustrated, your outer world will reflect frustration back to you. If there never seems to be enough money, look at what you were taught at home about money. Was lack the predominant pattern at home? "Money doesn't grow on trees." Remember that one? Look also at your giving. You need to look at every level of giving. Are you generous? Would your family or friends describe you as giving? Are you generous with your money, time, forgiveness, love, consideration, etc.? Get into action, giving more of everything that you have, and give what you want to get. Look at all the areas above, love, time, forgiveness, consideration, appreciation, praise, acknowledgement, etc. Would you like to have more of all of those things? Get into action, giving what you want to get.

TIP:

If you are always worried that there isn't enough, there won't be.

One of the Universal Laws is "You can't give what you don't have." Research Tithing. All of the most successful people tithe! John D. Rockefeller's first tithe was $9.00. He ended his life having tithed over $500,000,000. And don't forget, he started in the 1800's and died in the early 1900's. What would that be worth in today's dollars? When asked about his wealth, he would say, "GOD gave me my money." If you begin tithing, even if you think you do not have the funds to do it, the universe will support your decision because you must have it to give it. You are "acting as if." Start with giving 10% of what you have left after paying everything, including yourself. The theory of tithing is that you are honoring a higher power. Tithing says that you have faith that you will be taken care of. After all, even the smallest creatures on earth are taken care of, why not you? Money will begin to appear for you. I started tithing 10% of my net pay almost three years ago. During my health challenge, I was out of work for six months. I had over $24,000 come in the mail to me from people who had heard of my circumstances in just over three months. I did not need disability insurance (and I did not have any). Today I tithe 10% of my gross pay, 20% of my training and speaking events, and 30% of my book sales. Each year I add more and more income and I give out more and more. There is always plenty to spare and share. I figure that I did not come here with any money and I will not leave with any, so I must be here to manage it and have fun with it, and I do. Give what you want to get.

CHAPTER 17: MOTIVATE, MOTIVATE, MOTIVATE

Read everything pertaining to sales and to personal growth as a way to keep your motivation high. Read about how the Universe works and how successful people have a Higher Power in their life. Read *Think and Grow Rich, and the Universal Laws of Success* by Napoleon Hill. Read *As a Man Thinketh* by James Allen. Read books by Wayne Dyer, Deepak Chopra, Mark Victor Hansen, Jack Canfield and Jim Rohn. Read books on selling, like *The Sales Bible and the Little Red Book of Selling* by Jeffrey Gittomer. Read *Selling is Dead* by Marc T. Miller and Jason M. Sinkovitz.

And read *The Power of a Positive No* by William Ury and *The World's Greatest Salesman* by Og Mandino

TIP:

"Motivate yourself and lead by example to motivate those around you"

Develop your relationship with your Higher Power, as you define it. God, The Universe, The Divine, however you see the energy all around us, see it as a way to understand why you are here, and motivating yourself will be easy. You can leave all the hard stuff to your Higher Power and do what is on your plate to do in each moment. Leave the rest up to Her or Him.

Read biographies about successful people or about anyone you admire -- absorb them and consider adding to your own personality, a trait or strategy you found interesting. If it worked for others, why not give it a try. If you will not read, isn't that the same as someone who cannot read? Isn't the long term effect the same? Books on tape, CD, an iPOD or MP3 are the same thing. Just find a way to do it.

Buy the books. Buy the one day or two day seminars to get incremental changes in your behavior. Invest in reinforcement training that pertains to behavioral and attitude training -- not techniques only. This type of training is usually conducted over a long period of time. They vary from 12 weeks to 3 years or more. If you own or owned a company, or are employed as a salesperson, you are challenged today to motivate your sales support team to help you reach your goals. Teach, train, build, and respect your support staff. Listen to them. Push the cart, don't whip the ox. Help them help you get where you want to go. Include them, perhaps in the success. I've heard many salespeople say, "It's their job. They get paid to support me and it's what I expect." True, but do you think their support team went the extra mile for them. No way. Find a way to make it fun. Find a way for your team to get a win. Everyone loves winning. Sports teams know the objective with each game and they know who won in the end. Come up with something your support team can win daily, weekly, or monthly. Give them a reason to cheer and celebrate the win if they achieve it.

Have integrity. Do what you say. Your employees are watching and will know in an instant if you say one thing and do another.

Don't forget the losses. But review them in a blame proof atmosphere and remind your team that they take the field again tomorrow. A win is only around the corner. Have a crew of committed others to support you.

Acknowledge and praise them. Send them notes of appreciation and thank you's. Ask them what they would like in a gift and send them the gift; whatever it takes to let them know that you care. If people know you care, you can demand more.

CHAPTER 18: DREAM AND BELIEVE IN POSSIBILITIES

That's right. Dream, daydream, picture yourself where it is you want to be. Dream it. Believe it. Do it. Use your imagination machine. Use your imagination power to manifest your deepest desires.

Visualize the goal and the rewards of achieving it. Spend some time alone -- at the beach, in the woods, wherever you find peace, -- and see yourself doing what you want. Imagine yourself with the rewards of dream -- the big boat, the fame, the power, the money, whatever you want -- be there, at your goal, in your dreams. Imagine yourself with the family love and support. Imagine yourself satisfied with what you have. Be grateful. Feel what it feels like to always be grateful. The most successful people in sports visualize the outcome they want.

Do it. Selling will become easier when you see your outcomes first.

TIP:

Whatever it is you hope to achieve - Dream it.

To assist your visualizing process, spend some quiet time each day if you can or at least weekly. Create an image book that has pictures, quotes, affirmations, incantations and words that support your goals. Look at it twice daily, once when you first get up and once before you go to sleep. Studies have shown these times to be the most powerful times to impress anything on your subconscious mind. Begin to "act as if" you were already what you wanted to become and act like you already have what you wanted to have.

If satisfaction and fulfillment in life is your number one goal, begin to act as if you were satisfied and fulfilled already. My teacher, Toni Stone says that "Satisfaction is first a decision, feelings follow." She teaches that if one is not satisfied now, then they will never be satisfied later. They will always be satisfied.... when? When this happens or that happens, that is when they will be satisfied. The key is to be satisfied now, so that you will always be in a satisfied state of mind. There is no in between, if you are not satisfied, you will never be satisfied. Make the decision now, be satisfied.

Intention and visualization work together to help us manifest our deepest desires. Get the book, *The Power of Intention* by Wayne Dyer. Use visualization along with intending what you desire daily. Rent the movie "What the Bleep Do We Know and The Secret". Study the Law of Attraction. Your thoughts, words and actions have power. Einstein said that "There is no power greater than the power of imagination." Imagine yourself succeeding, dream dreams beyond where your mortal mind tells you is possible. Have that "BHAG" goal, as Mark Victor Hansen recommends, that "Big Hairy Audacious Goal." Why not? You can imagine anything. Feel what it would feel like to arrive at your goal. See the celebration. All of these steps contribute towards you reaching your goal.

Visualization has great power to bring one quicker to where one wants to go.

DREAM ON

By Stephen P. Lentini
Dream on, don't quit,
Dreamers seem to never fit.
They're off to lands,
We know not where,
But then again we'll never dare.
Believe you must! Is what they say,
Soon will come a golden day.
Never ever lose sight of it. Please. Please. Don't ever quit.
Keep on dreamin', it's what

you must, if you'll ever see what you think just

"I have no patience with people who are always raising difficulties," said Winston Churchill.

Possibilities, on the other hand, are another story. I cannot say for sure, although it's a safe bet that Churchill preferred people who believed in possibilities.

Each occurrence in our life holds a new opportunity, whether it is for personal or monetary growth. By always looking for the possibilities for growth, growth will come. Believe it.

TIP: Even during your most difficult times, look for possibilities and opportunities.

Your imagination knows no limits. Imagine your future. Napoleon Hill and Ernest Holmes once said that "You would not have the desire for something if you did not have the ability to bring it forth." If you feel a desire to achieve something special in your life, imagine it and feel what it feels like to have already achieved it, and then get on to doing it.

CHAPTER 19: INTEGRITY: KEEP YOUR WORD AND DO WHAT YOU SAID

How can you expect your clients to be impeccable with their word if you are not impeccable with your own? As a professional sales person, you are responsible for helping your prospects be impeccable with their word. When you hear a prospect use words that sound wishy-washy, it is your job to call them on it. What I use as my guide is "No lie goes by me un-addressed." How about your company or with your boss? Are you willing to be the stand for integrity with your company or your boss?

For example, if a client or prospect says, "You are looking good on this project" or "You are real close", you might say, "I appreciate the fact that we are close", "Sometimes when I have heard we are close in the past, it has turned out to mean that we were not getting the order. That is probably not the case here, is it?"

How can you call people on their wishy-washy words if you use them yourself? Listen to the words others around you use for the next two weeks. See if you can spot the times where you could ask, "What do you mean when you say …….?"

Better yet, listen to your own words. Are you wishy-washy with those around you? Are you often less than direct with people to soften the effect of what you are saying? Do you make promises you have no intention of keeping? If you are not impeccable with your own words, you will never hold those around you accountable for what they say, least of all, a prospect.

Do you have integrity?

Can you be counted on to keep your word? Ask others how you show up, how do they view you when it comes to keeping your word? Ask them to rate you on a scale of 1 – 10. Ask your spouse or significant other. Ask your Boss.

Clean up any lack of integrity that you find in yourself. Remember that you reap what you sow. What are you sowing with your word? I worked at a company where an issue came up with a former client. The client had just left the company where he was a member. It was a group organization. I had promised him that he qualified for our special program that would pay him an extra 1% of the monies that he had received over the previous 12 months. It would mean $13,000+ to his company. I checked with my boss at the time of the special request and she too gave her word that he did, in fact, qualify for our special program. When he left our group, my boss and the President of the company did not want to pay him because he had lied about whether he was staying with us as a member of the group. Regardless, we gave our word and I told my boss and the President that "It did not work for me that we were not going to keep our word," and that my request was that we pay him. It took six weeks of discussion, and eventually my boss and the President of the company agreed that it was more important to keep our word with this guy, even though he lied. I understood the emotions and all the feelings about being lied to by this member, and still, we gave our word. Our integrity and my own integrity were worth more than the $13,000+ -- it was priceless. Take a stand for integrity, even if you lose your job over it; would you want to be working for a company that breaks its word and is willing to put a price on its integrity?

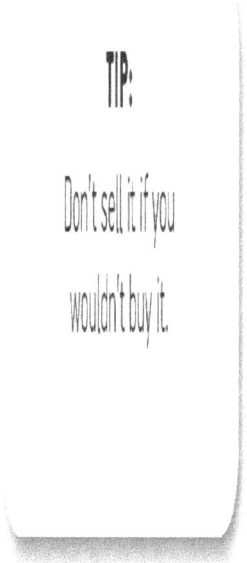

TIP: Don't sell it if you wouldn't buy it.

Don't sell more than someone needs to fill your bank account. Help your prospects buy, listen to what their needs are, and make sure that they are a good fit for your company or that what you sell is a good solution for them. If you have integrity, you will be sure to recommend that they buy something else or from someone else if they are not a fit. You have integrity if that is what you do. If you sell only to take care of your bank account, you will always be working hard to fill it. If you oversell someone, eventually they discover it. How do you think they feel about you? How do they feel about your company? What do you think they will tell others about you?

Your lack of integrity will catch up with you; what goes around comes around. Remember the law of cause and effect. Have integrity, if you take good care of others with integrity, they will gladly take care of your bank account . They will tell others, and your circle of cash will grow by referral. You will not have to worry about the future if you take great care of the present moment. If you are experiencing difficulties now, it is because of your lack of integrity during sometime past. Forget it and start cleaning it up now. Start doing the right thing now. Have integrity and the Universe and your customers will reward that effort.

CHAPTER 20: STOP THE WHINING AND START THE WINNING

I've met and worked with salespeople who whined more than a 6-year-old who wanted that new toy. The time that they spent whining could have been spent calling a new prospect for an appointment. I had no patience for these people because their whining sapped my energy. Stay away from whiners -- they sap your energy. If you are a whiner, stop. Use the energy for winning. Think of all that time you have spent whining, as wasted. You could have been selling. As soon as you catch yourself whining, stop it. Gradually, this stupid habit will disappear and you will see that you have more time for selling and winning.

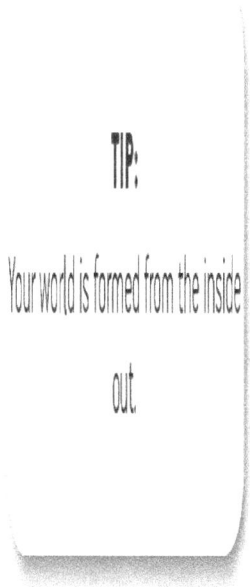

TIP:

Your world is formed from the inside out.

Your world is an outer picturing of your predominant thought patterns. Negative thinking creates a negative experience. If you don't like your experience of the world, change how the world is experiencing you.

You are the only one in this life that you can control. As you change, things will change. Track your responses to the people and events in your life. Where are you reacting the same way over and over and expecting a different outcome? Step back from those people, prospects, bosses, family, etc. and think about what would be a new response for you. What would be something new to say or do? When you do, you will start to see a new life form right before your eyes and the only one who changed was you.

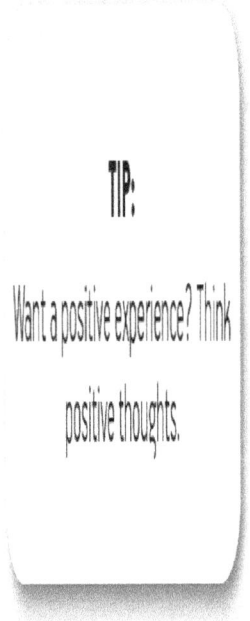

TIP: Want a positive experience? Think positive thoughts.

Good selling requires a lot of energy. Great selling requires even more. So guard your energy levels by staying positive, and keeping away from negative people. This includes customers, co-workers, bosses, and spouses – whomever.

If you are working in a negative company, get out. Move on -- there's a big world out there and a life beyond the company you are at. If the company cannot support your efforts, first find a way to support your company. Suggest new ways of doing things. Complain with a request or suggestion. If this does not work, find a new company.

Usually, negative people are unable to change. This is who they are and how they view the world.

Surround yourself with people who see possibilities and let no one put obstacles up between you and your goals. Once you have your goals set, guard your energy. Say it out loud. Practice saying "Sorry – believing it cannot happen or that we are blocked in any way from succeeding does not work for me." "Can we focus on what would work or how to get around this temporary obstacle?"

TIP:
Remind yourself frequently "Your energy is one of your most important assets."

You will find yourself identifying time and energy-draining people and customers, and successfully avoiding them. Selling will be a lot easier and more fun.

I know it's an old cliché but - refuse to let negative thoughts into your mind. Try picturing a door in your mind and when a negative thought enters, close the door, say "Thank you for sharing" and close the door.

Use affirmations! Anything that follows the words "I am" is an affirmation. You are the programmer of your mind. Listen to the words you are currently using in your everyday conversations. You will be amazed to hear some of the things that you are programming. Be clear, direct and concise in your words, and amazing things will follow.

Think about all the negative events in your life? Did you think about them casually before they happened? Did you ever casually wish for something that appeared later in your life?

TIP:

"Speak about what's intended, that's a way to win"

When you can see that you have created all the negative events in your life, you will see your own power to create. You will see just how powerful you are. Be intentional with your thoughts and words. Have them match what you long for. Whatever is your deepest longing, go for it. Eleanor Roosevelt once said, "You must do what you think you cannot do!" Be intentional with your thinking and speaking. Remember, you have created your world up until now without disciplined thinking or a focused effort.

> **TIP:**
>
> Just think what a powerful future you could create if you disciplined your thoughts and focused your efforts totally on your deepest desires.

Listen carefully to what you speak about. Journal your thoughts for a week, month, a quarter or a year or more. You will see that you are the creator of your circumstances. You are not at the effect of your circumstances. You are a powerful co–creator of your world. I say co-creator because I believe in a higher power in my life. I think about the fact that we live in a galaxy, in a Universe. I believe that I can tap into that power to create what I deeply desire. You can too. I have a coach and the support of others to help me stay on track. Disciplined and focused. I am achieving my deepest desires, you can too.

CHAPTER 21: BE GRATEFUL

It is not enough to think to yourself "well, I am grateful" once in a while.

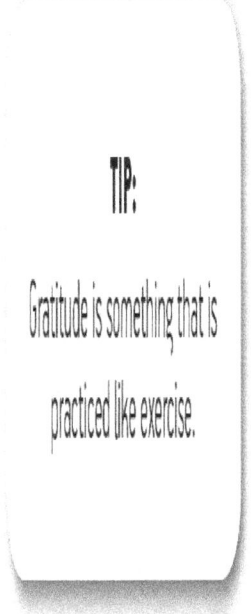

TIP:

Gratitude is something that is practiced like exercise.

To really see results in your life, you must be in gratitude for everything. Because I have been studying gratitude for many years and been speaking and writing what I was grateful for, I have prospered in ways that were once unimaginable to me. By speaking of gratitude and developing an awareness of being in a state of gratitude, I learned just how resentful and bitter I was without realizing it. When I started by actually saying out loud what I was grateful for, my brain would respond with "you're not grateful, who are you kidding?" I was surprised to learn just how ungrateful I really was.

As I said earlier, one afternoon, I was training a group of sales people. One second I was fine and the next, I needed an ambulance. While I was being attended to by the EMT's, I was saying how grateful I was for the experience. I know they must have thought that I was crazy, but I knew that great things were coming to me at that moment. I knew that this health challenge was the flood and the forest fire in my life. I had asked God "to clear the path" for me, so that I would clearly see what was mine to do in this world. Within a month or so, the health challenge appeared. Little did I know then that it was to be a six-month ordeal. I was in the hospital for 60 days straight, and over half of the next 2 months, for a total of 100 days. It would take almost a year before I would return to normal. Even on the way to Intensive Care, I was grateful. My whole life has changed since, and gratitude is the key. The whole time seemed like just a few days. And yes, I had a few blue moments and there were tears, but they only lasted hours, sometimes just minutes. Imagine, I could have been bitter for the whole experience.

TIP:
Practice Gratitude. Say what you are grateful for and write it every day.

You will become grateful even for what you currently define as awful, because you will see it as a gift later because of gratitude. Try it and see. Call or write me with your experiences.

CHAPTER 22: WE DO LIVE IN A GALAXY, IN A UNIVERSE

Take some quiet time each day, preferably 6am and 6pm, to reflect on the fact that we live in a Galaxy, in a Universe. During my health challenge, I had a moment in intensive care that truly changed the rest of my life. I was in the hospital for a little over four days, since Wednesday, and on Monday afternoon my friend Warren and my significant other, Janice, (now my soon to be wife), were visiting me. I remember seeing Janice and Warren one second, being in the hospital room with them, and the next second I was in another room, a large room. There were a lot of people in the room. I remember hearing and seeing someone speaking at the front of the room. I remember thinking, "Oh someone is speaking, I better move closer to hear what they are saying." I moved closer and realized that it was someone that I worked with that was speaking, Ken Foscaldo. Ken was giving a eulogy and this person had touched a lot of lives. I remember thinking, "Oh, this person has touched a lot of lives. I wonder who it is. I better move closer to hear who it is." In the next second, I realized that it was my own eulogy. Next I was asked, very gently, very lovingly, "Stay or go?" That was it, nothing else. I remember in that moment feeling very peaceful and thinking "Well, I have touched a lot of lives. Thy will be done." I surrendered my life to the will of the Universe, God or the Divine Consciousness. In that next second, I was back in the hospital room. When I was comfortable with sharing that story some weeks later with Warren and Janice, Warren mentioned that "It must have been Monday. The doctor had asked us to contact your family as it did not look good."

I am certain that one of the reasons that I came back is to share this story that we are always safe, connected to the Divine, the Universe, and living a miracle, as well as living in a miracle, in every moment. And that we have nothing to fear. To encourage people to live from the level of their soul and not the material world.

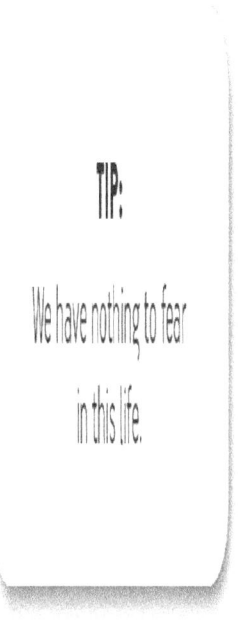

TIP:

We have nothing to fear in this life.

I have since remembered, not perfectly mind you, to surrender when I think that things are out of control. That I have nothing to fear since I have faced death, and that even in death, we have nothing to fear. We are safe, always and in every moment. At the moment of my death, there was no mention of anything I had achieved or failed to achieve. There was no mention of anything that I had acquired, nothing material at all. The only mention was of the people I had touched.

How many of us live working hard to achieve, and never stop to really be with and touch the people in our lives? How many of us really care, in each moment, of the other person in front of us? How many of us are only thinking of a quota or a promotion or the praise and accolades we will receive if we can "just close this customer?"

Take the time to really be with your customers and prospects. Really feel what you are feeling and work to help your customers and prospects find the best solution for them, even if it is not you. You get what you give and the Universe will reward you.

When you look up in the sky at night, we too are just one of those little twinkling stars. Physicists and astronomers, with the help of the Hubble telescope, confirm now that just in our galaxy alone there are over 200 billion suns with planets that circle them. That's in our galaxy alone! We live in a miracle. Take time each day to reflect on that and remember to bring miracle thinking with you in each moment. The Universe is infinite, so bring some infinite possibility thinking with you as well. Imagine the energy that someone who thinks this way brings to every moment.

I salute the Divine in each person, silently, and send them my blessings as a gift. This helps me to detach from the outcome and to remember that I do live in a Galaxy, in a Universe.

Don't worry about your quotas. Keep making sales calls, looking to help people buy, and be fully present with them, intending to help them, and you will be successful. I have been. Deepak Chopra, says in his book *Power, Freedom and Grace*, "As you elevate your attention from the world of the humdrum and trivial to the world of the magical and miraculous, your life becomes magical and miraculous. Your attention is spontaneously alert to the fact that life itself is a miracle. And the more you put your attention on miracles, the more you become the conscious creator of miracles"

I urge you to bring your attention up to the level of the Divine -- the miraculous in every moment -- even in those moments when someone or something is bothersome, difficult or even tragic. We cannot always see the miracle immediately or the reason for these difficult moments, and usually some time later, we can see why they happened or how they contributed immensely to our growth, to our lives.

TIP:

Thoughts have energy, so think about what you are sending to others with your thinking, and think about bringing a miracle with you.

Try it for two or three years and see if you live a more joyful, successful, satisfied life.

Some stories of success;

My best and most memorable sales started at *no*.

1. HARVARD UNIVERSITY

My best and most memorable sales started at no. I remember, as I write this, my first call with a sales rep that worked for me at Harvard University. The buyer, Linda Zedros, started our appointment with "We could never buy from you." I said, "Oh, I'm a little confused then, why did we get the appointment?"

I was very confused at that moment. Wouldn't you be? I like to pay attention to what I am feeling and what I notice about the buyer's body language or facial expressions. I then find a way to say what I am feeling or noticing.

Linda replied to my question "Oh, we heard a lot about your company and since you're new to Massachusetts, I figured we would find out about you."

I replied, "Oh, what did you hear?" She told me. I then asked, "Linda, since we are not going to get the business, would you mind telling me all about what you are looking for and why we cannot get the business?"

Linda replied, "We currently have 16 suppliers and with some we have done business for over 30 years...so you see we could never give the business to you, we have never even done any business and we are going to select one supplier from the 16 and consolidate all of our purchases."

I said, "That makes sense...it's probably what I would do."... "Would you mind telling me about your process of selection and what you are looking for the finalist to do for you?"

She replied, "Sure, no problem."

Linda went on to tell me all about her process, what she was looking for her selected supplier to give her, etc. I spent over 45 minutes talking with someone who told me that we did not have a chance.

I ended our call with "You know Linda, it sounds to me like you're looking for a supplier partner." and she replied, "Oh, partnership, what do you mean, would you explain that?" I replied, "Well, aren't all of your suppliers going to be coming in to your review and selection process?" Linda replied "yes." I said, "Why don't you wait and see if your current suppliers have the same idea and if not, call me. I'll be glad to share it with you." She agreed that was fair.

Two weeks later, I got a phone call from Linda at Harvard, asking me to come in and explain my vision of a supplier partner. I said "Sure Linda, would you do me a favor?" She replied, "No problem, of course." I said, "Would you mind putting me on that list of suppliers that you are considering?"

She said, "Yes." Needless to say, I was on cloud nine that day.

Six months later, after a complete review of all the suppliers, and a bunch of work by a great team of people, WE GOT THE BUSINESS. THE COMPANY THAT LINDA SAID, "NO, WE COULD NEVER BUY FROM YOU."

We were awarded the contract for over $1,000,000 in annual sales!

2. SPAULDING AND SLYE.

Six months later, I met Peter Delucca of Spaulding and Slye Real Estate management at a BOMA cocktail party. He saw my name badge and said,

"Oh, your with XXXX Paper company, we could never buy from you.'" and I said to Peter, "How do you know that I would sell you?"

He was a little stunned and said, "Why wouldn't you sell us?" I asked him, "Do you sell everyone in your market?"He replied, "No." I said, "Why not?" Peter replied, "Well, not everyone is a fit…" and I asked " and that is because…"Peter replied, "Well, we cannot make money on every situation so we have to find out if we are a fit."

I said to Peter, "Well it's the same for us."He understood. We spoke the rest of the evening and exchanged cards. I asked him before we parted, "How come you said that you could never buy from us?" He said, "Oh, we have six or seven paper companies now and I am going to consolidate them to one and we have never even purchased from you."

Well, there is a lot more to the story, and guess what happened a few weeks later? That's right, I got the business…over $750,000 annually.

What's more, when I got to Boston one year earlier, I said to those around me "I am going to get Harvard and Spaulding & Slye."

Funny how things work out.

Contrary to popular belief, selling does not have to be difficult. In fact, we are all programmed by nature to succeed with the least effort. If you are having trouble maintaining or growing your sales and commissions, give the steps above a try. If you are still finding sales difficult, honestly and brutally review what you have been planting in the way of activity or integrity; you are reaping that harvest. Use this book to prepare a new harvest and start planting new seeds now, right now.

I wish you an abundant harvest. Start planting.

Remember, great things start at no. It takes the pressure off of everyone. You can say what's important and what's the truth.

I say go for no in your conversations with Prospects. You cannot lose what you do not have anyway.

Go get 20 no's today and 100 for the month, and see what happens.

I wish you good selling.

Gratefully yours, Steve

ABOUT AUTHOR

With more than 40 years of sales management experience, Stephen P. Lentini is the CEO of Lentini Sales Leadership and the Director of The Prosperity Institute, a business consulting and training company in Taunton, MA and Johnson, VT. He writes, teaches and trains on a variety of sales and management topics for audiences nationwide and has just completed work on his first in a series of sales books titled *Sales Success for Rookies, How to Succeed at Sales Right From the Start* a book and CD program. The next book in the series is *Sales Success for Veteran Sales People, How to Stay at Peak Performance*.

He is currently writing, teaching and developing other books, including *Wake up, Jump into your Life, Twenty Strategies for a Life of Joy, Universal Selling*, and *Integrating the Culture of Change, Sales Success for the Spiritual Sales Person, how to sell without losing your soul* and others. Steve can be reached at 917-805-1088 or email at steve@stevelentini.com

www.ingramcontent.com/pod-product-compliance
Lightning Source LLC
Chambersburg PA
CBHW050009230526
45465CB00003BB/1332